FROM TRAUMA TO ENLIGHTENMENT

THE FOUR STEPS TO UNCONDITIONAL SELF-ACCEPTANCE

FROM TRAUMA TO ENLIGHTENMENT

THE FOUR STEPS TO UNCONDITIONAL SELF-ACCEPTANCE

BY DR. BRIAN ALMAN
WITH CONTRIBUTIONS AND ENDORSEMENT BY DR. VINCENT FELITTI

STORYTELLER MEDIA

Copyright © 2025 Dr.Brian Alman
All rights reserved.

Published by Storyteller Media, Publishers Matthew Medney & Charles Allen

Storyteller Media and its logo are trademarks of Storyteller Media LLC, A joint venture with Gungnir Entertainment LLC

Cover design by GUNGNIR ENTERTAINMENT

ISBN 9798999529985

Edited by Charles Allen

Publisher and wholesale enquiries:
www.storyteller.media

Distributed by macmillan

Printed in Canada

First Edition: 2025

TABLE OF CONTENTS

Introduction	01
Part One: Awareness	10
Chapter 1	11
Chapter 2	14
Chapter 3	27
Chapter 4	40
Part Two: Understanding	46
Chapter 5	47
Chapter 6	51
Chapter 7	55
Part Three: Release	64
Chapter 8	65
Chapter 9	70
Chapter 10	73
Part Four: Integration	76
Chapter 11	77
Chapter 12	85
Final Thoughts	89
Bonus Chapter	93

INTRODUCTION

I'd like to take some time here to tell you a little bit about how this book, From Trauma to Enlightenment, came about. It's quite a long story, and I will make it simple and direct, although I will give you some of the details, so you understand this book's evolution, the story behind it, why it was written, and for whom.

Well, I was born missing part of my back, part of L4 and L5 vertebrae. So, I had chronic back pain as a kid and as a teen. Growing up, I did what most people do with chronic pain. You go to the medical doctor, orthopedic surgeon, physical therapy, try medications—all kinds of different practitioners because, basically, you try everything because pain is a full-time job. It impacts everything. It's debilitating. And I kept reading about pain, pain experts, pain doctors, everywhere in the world.

I read everything I could, and one name kept coming up, Dr. Milton Erickson, who got into the field of pain because of his own pain. He had polio as a teenager and wasn't even supposed to make it past his teens. I met him when he was 75 years young, and he'd written a lot of books, read a lot of articles, and really was the most brilliant person I read about. I was fascinated with him when it came to him dealing with his own pain and teaching other people about how to deal with theirs. So, I wrote him a handwritten letter and told him my story, the same story that I just told you, and asked if he would be willing to train me. He wrote me back a handwritten letter and said he would train me if I got a PhD in psychology or an MD degree.

I really didn't want to get a PhD in psychology or an MD degree. I really wanted to help myself deal with my pain and then help other people deal with theirs. I wrote him back saying as such, but when he responded again, he only repeated what he'd said before.

I was in my last year of college at the time, so I started applying to PhD psychology programs. Fortunately, I got into a school in San Diego for a master's degree and PhD degree, which I then did. During those four years, I traveled back and forth to Phoenix where his office was located. I was a very devoted student and the youngest student, the only one without a degree, sort of like the runt of the litter or the punk with the least experience. People wondered, *Why is he here?*

But we had a special connection, Dr. Erickson and me. We had both gotten into the practice because of our pain. I knew that was important, but I wouldn't realize that until many years later. So, I was learning mind-body healing. I was learning medical hypnosis, meditation, mindfulness, all kinds of positive psychology, all kinds of different approaches. In these group sessions and private sessions, I went from being a student to being a patient because, and this was quite unfortunate, my mother got ALS (Amyotrophic Lateral Sclerosis) while I was getting my training. She was back in Massachusetts where we were all from. And so, all of a sudden, I was dealing with the most horrendous experience. Anybody that knows about ALS understands it's just a complete deterioration of somebody in their late forties who had been vibrant at the peak of their life just a year before that.

Dr. Erickson was incredibly helpful to me when I was going through that. And in addition to going from a student to a patient, he was kind enough to be a collaborator. He helped me write my first book, which became very popular and was translated into a number of different languages. He helped me get an opportunity to teach at the University of California at San Diego. That worked out fantastic. I did that for a number of years, and he helped me write my first medical journal article, which was also quite popular at the time. So, I got quite a bit of training. He even let me work with patients he was working with. Of course, they would say, why is he here? Meaning me. But he was training me, and he thought I could be helpful.

It was quite a relationship, quite extraordinary. I was very fortunate, and I was a highly motivated student. I would read anything, I'd practice anything, I'd study everything. After about a year and a half of the training, I realized I just wasn't understanding the training in the same way that other trainees were learning the methods. I was distracted. My mind was busy. I tried to relax. I tried self-hypnosis, meditation, and mindfulness, but my mind was so busy.

I would be so critical of myself, constantly doubting and running inner monologues, *Are you doing it right? Are you sure you know what you're doing? Everybody looks like they know what they're doing. Are you doing it as well? Are you doing it wrong? Are you ever going to get this?*

So, I was really concerned. And, of course, I shared that with Dr. Erickson because he was a master with himself and with other people. In the morning, he was in a lot of pain. So, he'd go practice his own sessions and an hour later, he would come out looking youthful and energetic. It was a really amazing transformation.

Later in the day around 3, 4, 5 o'clock, he'd start to maybe look a little bit tired, maybe not feel as well, and have some more discomfort, which is what we learned to call "the pain." He'd go into his room for another hour. He'd come out, and he was bright-eyed. Of course, later on, I built up the courage to ask him what he did during that hour because, of course, I wanted to know and practice that for myself. But more importantly, I was asking him, what can I do about quieting my mind to be able to be meditative, to be able to get into the self-hypnosis state?

The main technique with meditation, mindfulness, self-hypnosis, prayer psychology, art, and music is to step back and be the observer, be the watcher. Just be the person who is observing you because that third person perspective is really a good perspective. It will help you understand yourself much better. It's a great technique in all the meditations and all the different approaches, all the eastern and western traditions combined. But my observer, my watcher, my witness was just too busy. So I worked on it day and night, and one night, in the middle of the night, about a year and a half into my training, I had an epiphany. It was life changing.

In an instant, I became much more relaxed. I was suddenly able to experience what I hadn't been able to experience. It was a tremendous breakthrough, definitely the biggest change I had ever felt psychologically, emotionally, mentally, or even physically. I was so excited. I called Dr. Erickson immediately after the breakthrough and told him about what I experienced and my life changing epiphany. He said, "Brian, can you call back in a couple hours? It's five in the morning. Call back at seven."

So, I did, and we started working on expanding that epiphany, and developing the core concepts so that I could help other people learn from those understandings. We will discuss the fully evolved versions of these practices, and you will be able to master them and make them your own personal epiphanies throughout our time together in this book. Before we get there though, to continue the story, while I was working directly with Dr. Erickson, I started working at Kaiser Permanente with a person named Vincent Felitti, another medical doctor who was just getting his adverse childhood experiences (ACE) study going. He was very interested in what I was doing with mind body healing. He really liked my book and my medical journal article. He asked me if I would come and work with him and help the people that he was working with. At Kaiser, the department that he was the head of, was seeing 25,000 people per year, and the adverse childhood experiences, the ACE study, grew out of that. And I became the treatment solution, founder, and director with Dr. Felitti for the ACE study.

Now, during this time, I also realized my back pain and the loss of my mother at a young age was an ACE. It was emotional, it was psychological, it was physical, it was a trauma. I was traumatized. So, I was quite motivated to work with Dr. Felitti. He got into the field because of his own ACEs. We have been collaborating on a weekly basis for decades now. And one of the big results of this is what you'll be reading, *From Trauma to Enlightenment*.

Now, how did we get the name? I was invited to go to India to teach people that are at Ashrams in India to go deeper into meditation. They had read my book, *Self-Hypnosis*. They had read some of my other books, including, Your Inner Voice. That was amazing to me. Here I was, a person from Massachusetts and living in California, going to India to teach people how to go deeper in meditation because they discovered my books on the other side of the world. They had been meditating for decades, probably generations, so it was beyond an honor to get to share my techniques and perspectives on the subject.

I went because, in addition to teaching there, I was also interested to find out if anybody was *really* enlightened. I was curious and wanted to know what that meant, enlightenment. Sure, I could be enlightened for fifteen minutes. I could be enlightened for a little bit of time, be in the zone, be in the flow, but it didn't last. I'm a parent. For those of you who are, you know, that will sure take you out of it at times! I also have responsibilities and priorities, and those will take you out of it. But maybe there is somebody who is always in the zone, always in the flow, *enlightened*. So, I went, and I traveled, and I met brilliant women, brilliant men, and amazing colleagues. I learned so much from the people there, but I really didn't meet anybody that was enlightened.

So, I thought, *Okay, well, I met brilliant people. They're amazing. I hope I know them for the rest of my life.* And as I was leaving, the last person I was teaching with said to me, *Well, what do you think enlightenment is? I told him, It's transcendence, always in the zone, always relaxed, and can deal with anything. Ethereal, above it all.* And the person said, *No. I said, Uh oh.* So, I've been to India, I've been traveling around. I've done all this teaching, and I have the wrong definition. Oh my goodness. Now what am I going to do? He said, *Enlightenment is unconditional acceptance of yourself.*

Wow. That's what my dozen books are about. That's what my videos are about. That is what my programs are about. My courses, everything I do, all my sessions, all the work I do, all the work at Kaiser Permanente, everything we've been doing with our studies, and our research has always been about teaching people these skills. Resolve the root causes, resolve the root issues, and learn the necessary skills so you can integrate them into your daily life. So, I renamed my app, Enlightn. This book, therefore, became *From Trauma to Enlightenment*.

So now you understand why. You understand the journey of how. I really hope this book enhances your journey of transformation, your ever evolving life, toward greater health and happiness so that you can expand your contribution to the world. So that you can make it a better place while you develop your unconscious self and your inner potential—your true authentic self. Let's begin with a brief overview of how we will embark on this journey together through the pages of this book.

INTRODUCTION

THE ACE STUDY, THE TRAUMA REVOLUTION, AND THE PROFOUND IMPACTS

We all carry stories. Some stories we wear proudly on the surface, and others are buried deep within us, beneath the layers of our everyday lives. These hidden stories often stem from the most painful and defining moments of our past, shaping how we see the world, see ourselves, and interact with others. For many, these stories are the echoes of trauma.

Trauma is a word that resonates deeply in the modern world. Its impact is far-reaching, affecting our mental, emotional, and physical health. But what if I told you that trauma, while undeniably painful, does not have to define who you are? What if I told you there is a path to healing and embracing yourself fully—unconditionally, in all your complexity and beauty? This is the path I will guide you through in *Trauma to Enlightenment: The Four Steps to Unconditional Self-Acceptance.*

The journey from trauma to self-acceptance is not easy. It demands courage, vulnerability, and a willingness to confront parts of ourselves that we may have long ignored or suppressed. But the potential for healing lives within each of us. This book is about accessing that potential.

I wrote this book not with decades of experience in trauma recovery but also as someone who has witnessed firsthand the transformative power of self-acceptance. Over the years, I've worked with countless individuals—each with their own stories, pain, and hope for something more. This book reflects that work, offering a step-by-step process to guide you through the most challenging aspects of healing from trauma.

The framework I present is simple but profound:

1. **Awareness** – The first step is to become aware of the stories that have shaped you. What beliefs have you carried since childhood? What experiences have defined how you view yourself? Awareness is the foundation of all healing.

2. **Understanding** – Once we are aware, we must dive deeper to understand the root of our pain. This step is about connecting the dots between past experiences and present challenges, allowing us to understand what happened.

3. **Release** – True healing requires letting go of what no longer serves us. In this stage, we will explore ways to release the emotional, mental, and physical burdens we have carried for far too long.

4. **Integration** – The final step is integrating these new understandings into our daily lives. It's about learning how to live in a way that reflects our true, authentic selves—free from the grip of trauma and filled with the peace of self-acceptance.

These four steps are grounded in one of the most significant studies on trauma: the Adverse Childhood Experiences (ACE) Study, led by Dr. Vincent Felitti in collaboration with the CDC. The ACE Study is one of the most groundbreaking pieces of research in the field of trauma recovery, forever transforming how we understand the impact of childhood adversity on adult well-being.

The ACE Study began in the 1990s and was revolutionary in its scope, linking early childhood trauma, such as abuse, neglect, and household dysfunction, to long-term health outcomes. What Dr. Felitti and our team discovered was startling: individuals who experienced adverse childhood experiences were significantly more likely to face a range of challenges later in life, including mental health issues, chronic disease, addiction, and difficulties in relationships. The study exposed the pervasive and lasting effects of trauma, showing that the body and mind carry these wounds far beyond childhood.

The findings of the ACE Study have had a profound global impact. Trauma-informed care, a model of care that acknowledges the widespread presence of trauma and its effects, is now a cornerstone of mental health and healing practices around the world. Healthcare professionals, educators, social workers, and mental health experts have embraced trauma-informed approaches that prioritize safety, trust, and empowerment—shifting away from judgment and blame and toward understanding and support.

This book incorporates the powerful insights of the ACE Study into a practical and accessible guide to self-healing. The research has not only transformed our understanding of trauma but has also inspired new approaches to healing that address the whole person, mind, body, and spirit. It highlights the importance of acknowledging our past but also empowers us to move beyond it, release the grip of trauma, and reclaim our lives with compassion.

In the following chapters, you will find explanations of these four steps and practical exercises, real-life stories, and clinically proven techniques to help you along the way. Whether you are a trauma survivor seeking healing, a mental health professional supporting others, or someone on a personal journey of self-discovery, this book is for you. Together, we will walk this path from trauma to enlightenment, learning how to embrace ourselves fully and completely—without conditions, judgment, and fear.

Let's begin this journey toward unconditional self-acceptance and discover the freedom beyond trauma.

FROM TRAUMA TO ENLIGHTENMENT

PART ONE: AWARENESS

CHAPTER 1

AWARENESS: THE FIRST STEP TO ENLIGHTENMENT THROUGH SELF-ACCEPTANCE

Awareness is the foundation of all healing. It's the first crucial step in the journey from trauma to unconditional self-acceptance because you cannot heal what you are unaware of. The painful experiences we've endured, particularly those from childhood, often shape our lives in ways that are hidden beneath the surface. We may feel anxiety, low self-esteem, or have relationship challenges, but rarely do we immediately connect these struggles to deep-rooted experiences of trauma. This chapter aims to guide you toward recognizing these hidden stories, illuminating their impact on you, and ultimately bringing them into the light of awareness.

WHAT IS AWARENESS?

At its core, awareness is the ability to observe yourself with clarity and honesty. It involves paying attention to your thoughts, emotions, and physical sensations in the present moment so you can further develop your capacity to be aware with less judgment and denial.

It's about noticing patterns in your behavior and understanding where they originate. When you develop awareness, you begin to see how past experiences—particularly those involving trauma—have shaped your beliefs, reactions, and how you view yourself.

Awareness requires a willingness to turn inward to confront, better understand, and help with the discomfort we often avoid. For trauma survivors, this can be incredibly challenging. Trauma frequently leaves us in a state of hypervigilance, constantly on guard and detached from the parts of ourselves that hold pain. But awareness is about gently opening the door to those parts of ourselves that we've neglected or pushed aside, allowing us to observe them compassionately.

CHAPTER 1

TRAUMA AND THE SUBCONSCIOUS MIND

The experiences of trauma can drive our thoughts and behaviors without us even knowing it. You may notice you frequently feel anxious or self-critical but do not fully understand why. Trauma creates internal narratives—messages we tell ourselves about who we are and what we deserve—that become ingrained over time. These narratives, rooted in childhood or past adversity, often go unnoticed, but they quietly influence our decisions, relationships, and self-esteem.

For example, a person who experienced emotional neglect as a child may have internalized the belief that they are unworthy of love or attention. This belief may manifest as difficulty forming intimate relationships or constant people-pleasing behaviors later in life. Without awareness, these behaviors can seem like random quirks or unchangeable traits, but once they are brought into conscious awareness, they can be examined, understood, and eventually transformed.

THE ROLE OF AWARENESS IN HEALING

Awareness allows you to step back from your automatic responses to life. Instead of reacting impulsively or being driven by subconscious beliefs, awareness will enable you to observe your reactions and choose how you want to respond. This is an incredibly liberating realization because it gives you control over your healing process. You can understand this as your ability to let go of some control to gain an even greater control.

When you cultivate awareness, you stop viewing yourself as a victim of circumstances and start seeing yourself as an active participant in your healing journey. You begin to notice your Inner Critic, those automatic negative thoughts about yourself, and instead of accepting them as truth, you can start to question them: "Where does this thought come from? Why do I feel unworthy at this moment? Is this belief mine, or is it a reflection of my past?"

This awareness lays the groundwork for more profound healing. You must become aware of your emotional burdens before you can understand and release them. By bringing your subconscious patterns to light, you can see how they have influenced your life and take the first steps toward breaking free from them.

THE POWER OF NON-JUDGMENTAL (UNCONSCIOUS) AWARENESS

As you begin to develop awareness, it's essential to approach this process with self-compassion. Awareness is not about continuing to criticize or judge yourself for the ways you've responded to trauma, conflict, difficult people and stressful situations. Self-judgment can hinder healing by reinforcing feelings of shame and inadequacy. Instead, strive to make progress so you can observe yourself with curiosity and kindness.

The purpose of awareness is to help you understand yourself more fully, not to blame or punish yourself for past mistakes. Trauma responses, whether they manifest as avoidance, self-sabotage, or overachievement, are often survival mechanisms. They were once necessary to protect you. As you develop deep, friendly, caring, and compassionate awareness, you can honor these survival strategies while recognizing that they may no longer serve you.

MOVING FORWARD

Awareness is the first essential step on the path to self-acceptance. It illuminates the patterns that have held you back and reveals the deeper truths behind your reactions. As you build your deeper awareness, you begin to see yourself more clearly. Not just through the lens of trauma but with a compassionate understanding of how your experiences have shaped you.

In the following chapters, I will introduce the ACE and PCE Assessments, briefly explain the ACE Study, and explain why it is vital to your trauma healing journey.

CHAPTER 2

AWARENESS WITH THE ACE ASSESSMENT

Childhood is supposed to be a time of innocence, growth, and safety, but for many, it is marked by adversity and trauma. These early experiences shape the mind and emotions and have long-lasting effects on the body and overall health. To fully understand how trauma impacts our lives, and how awareness of that trauma is the first step toward healing, we must look to one of the most groundbreaking studies in trauma research: the Adverse Childhood Experiences (ACE) Study.

The ACE Study, led by Dr. Vincent Felitti in partnership with the Centers for Disease Control and Prevention (CDC), revolutionized our understanding of the connection between childhood trauma and adult well-being. Its findings made it clear that the effects of childhood adversity are not confined to memory or emotion; they infiltrate our physical health, relationships, and mental resilience in ways that can shape an entire lifetime.

In this chapter, we'll explore the ACE Study, why taking the ACE Assessment can be a critical step toward gaining awareness of your own childhood traumas, and how this awareness forms the foundation for healing. The ACE framework is not just about understanding trauma, it's about shining a light on the hidden influences of the past and equipping you with the knowledge to begin your healing journey.

THE ACE STUDY: A GROUNDBREAKING INSIGHT INTO CHILDHOOD TRAUMA

The ACE Study began in the mid-1990s as a joint research project with Dr. Vincent Felitti and Dr. Robert Anda, examining how childhood trauma affects adult health and behavior. The study involved over 17,000 participants, mostly middle-class Americans, who were asked to provide detailed information about their childhood experiences, particularly those that involved emotional, physical, or sexual abuse, as well as family dysfunction like addiction, mental illness, or domestic violence.

After people answered the ACE questions, Dr. Felitti and Dr. Anda referred people to their ACE Treatment Solution Founder and Clinical Director, me!

After all, the results of the study were startling.

The researchers discovered that nearly two-thirds of participants had experienced at least one form of childhood trauma, and one in six had experienced four or more types of adverse childhood experiences. More importantly, the study revealed a direct correlation between the number of ACEs (Adverse Childhood Experiences) a person had and their likelihood of experiencing adverse health outcomes later in life. These outcomes included higher risks for chronic diseases like heart disease, diabetes, and cancer, as well as mental health issues such as depression, anxiety, addiction, and even early death.

This connection between childhood trauma and adult health painted a sobering picture: the more adversity a person faced in childhood, the greater their risk of struggling with health, relationships, and overall well-being as an adult. Trauma, it turned out, wasn't just something that happened in the mind. Trauma left a profound imprint on the body as well, influencing everything from stress hormones to immune function.

WHAT IS THE ACE ASSESSMENT?

At the heart of the ACE Study is the ACE Assessment, a simple but powerful questionnaire measuring the number of adverse experiences a person encountered during childhood. The assessment covers ten categories of trauma, including:

1. **Emotional Abuse** – Frequent yelling, insults, humiliation, or being made to feel unloved or unwanted.
2. **Physical Abuse** – Being physically hurt, threatened, or injured by a caregiver.
3. **Sexual Abuse** – Unwanted sexual contact or exposure to sexual acts.
4. **Emotional Neglect** – Feeling as though caregivers did not meet your emotional needs.

5. **Physical Neglect** – Not having basic needs like food, shelter, or medical care consistently met.
6. **Household Substance Abuse** – Living with a family member who had a problem with alcohol or drugs.
7. **Household Mental Illness** – Having a family member who struggled with mental health issues like depression or schizophrenia.
8. **Parental Separation or Divorce** – Growing up with separated or divorced parents.
9. **Domestic Violence** – Witnessing violence between parents or caregivers.
10. **Incarceration of a Family Member** – Having a parent or family member in jail or prison.

Each of these categories represents a different type of trauma that can profoundly affect a child's development. The ACE Assessment gives you a score based on how many of these experiences you encountered before age 18. A higher score indicates a greater risk of experiencing adverse health and emotional outcomes later in life.

WHY TAKING THE ACE ASSESSMENT IS A CRITICAL STEP IN HEALING

For many people, trauma is something that remains hidden, buried beneath the surface of daily life. Did you know that at least 70% of people globally will experience a potentially traumatic event during their lifetime. We may be aware of particular struggles, such as chronic anxiety, self-esteem issues, difficulty in relationships but the connection to childhood experiences may not be immediately apparent. The ACE Assessment offers a concrete way to begin uncovering these connections.

1. **Bringing Hidden Trauma to Light**
   One of the most powerful aspects of the ACE Assessment is that it forces you to reflect on your past in a structured way. You may uncover painful or difficult experiences you had previously minimized, forgotten, or downplayed by answering the questions. This process of identifying your ACEs is the first step toward awareness. Without this awareness, it is difficult to understand how your childhood has shaped your adult

life. Taking the ACE Assessment helps to bridge that gap, shining a light on the hidden patterns of trauma that may be influencing your mental, emotional, and physical well-being.

2. **Understanding Your ACE Score**
   While your ACE score is not the whole story of who you are, it is a valuable tool for understanding how your past may affect your present. A higher ACE score doesn't mean healing is impossible or you are destined for poor health or emotional challenges. However, it does mean that you may need to pay extra attention to how trauma has shaped your life and seek support in addressing these issues. Your ACE score is a starting point—a way of gaining clarity about the adversity you faced as a child so that you can begin to address its lingering effects.

3. **Validating Your Experiences**
   Many trauma survivors struggle with feelings of shame, guilt, or self-blame. They may minimize their experiences, telling themselves that what they went through "wasn't that bad" or that they should just "move on" from the past. The ACE Study offers validation. It provides scientific proof that what you experienced in childhood matters and has real, measurable impacts on your health and well-being. By taking the ACE Assessment, you can see your experiences not as isolated events but as part of a larger pattern that deserves attention and care.

4. **Building Awareness for Healing**
   Awareness is the foundation of healing, and the ACE Assessment is a critical tool for building that awareness. Once you understand your ACE score and the types of traumas you experienced, you can begin to see how those experiences may have influenced your beliefs, behaviors, and emotional patterns. This understanding allows you to start addressing the root causes of your struggles rather than just managing the symptoms. Whether it's anxiety, depression, relationship challenges, or physical health problems, understanding how your childhood shaped these issues is the first step toward healing.

5. **Mitigating Long-Term Effects of ACEs**
   The ACE Study revealed that ACEs are common and powerful in terms of their long-term effects on us as individuals, emotionally, bio-medically, and in terms of life expectancy. Taking the ACE assessment brings this to light so you can begin healing the root cause of your current symptoms of ACEs and mitigating any illness or disease that could develop from unaddressed ACEs.

BEYOND THE ACE SCORE: TRAUMA IS NOT DESTINY

It's important to remember that while your ACE score provides valuable insight into your past, it does not determine your future. Trauma may increase your risk for specific challenges, but it does not doom you to a lifetime of suffering. One of the most important findings of the ACE Study is that healing is possible, and that awareness is a critical part of that process.

The ACE Study also revealed that resilience factors, such as supportive relationships, safe environments, and access to mental health care, can help mitigate the effects of childhood trauma. While you cannot change the past, you can take steps in the present to create an environment of healing, safety, and support. The key to transforming trauma is not ignoring or denying it but instead becoming aware of its impact and actively working to address it.

MOVING FORWARD WITH AWARENESS

Taking the ACE Assessment is just the beginning of your healing journey. Once you've gained awareness of the trauma you experienced in childhood, the next step is to begin exploring how that trauma has influenced your life in more profound ways. In the following chapters, we will explore exercises and practices designed to help you increase self-awareness, identify trauma patterns, and begin the process of release and integration.

Remember, awareness is the foundation of healing. By taking the ACE Assessment, you are choosing to resolve and heal your past, not with fear or avoidance, but with courage and a commitment to your well-being. The road ahead may not always be easy, but with awareness as your guide, you are already on the path to unconditional self-acceptance and lasting healing.

THE ACE ASSESSMENT

Answer the following questions honestly. Then, calculate your number of "1" or "yes" responses. This is your ACE score.

Prior to your 18th birthday:

1. **Did a parent or other adult in the household often or very often**
   Swear at you, insult you, put you down, or humiliate you?
   Or
   Act in a way that made you afraid you might be physically hurt?
   Yes / No If yes, enter 1 _____

2. **Did a parent or other adult in the household often or very often**
   Push, grab, slap, or throw something at you?
   Or
   Ever hit you so hard that you had marks or were injured?
   Yes / No If yes, enter 1 _____

3. **Did an adult or person at least five years older than you ever**
   Touch or fondle you, or have you touch their body in a sexual way?
   Or
   Attempt or actually have oral, anal, or vaginal intercourse with you?
   Yes / No If yes, enter 1 _____

4. **Did you often or very often feel that**
   No one in your family loved you or thought you were important or special?
   Or
   Your family didn't look out for each other, feel close to each other, or support each other?
   Yes / No If yes, enter 1 _____

5. **Did you often or very often feel that**
   You didn't have enough to eat, had to wear dirty clothes, and had no one to protect you?
   Or
   Your parents were too drunk or high to take care of you or take you to the doctor if you needed it?
   Yes / No If yes, enter 1 _____

6. **Were your parents ever separated or divorced?**
   Yes / No If yes, enter 1 _____

7. **Was your mother or stepmother**
   Often or very often pushed, grabbed, slapped, or had something thrown at her?
   Or
   Sometimes, often, or very often kicked, bitten, hit with a fist, or hit with something hard?
   Or
   Ever repeatedly hit over at least a few minutes or threatened with a gun or knife?
   Yes / No If yes, enter 1 _____

8. **Did you live with anyone who was a problem drinker or alcoholic or who used street drugs?**
   Yes / No If yes, enter 1 _____

9. **Was a household member depressed or mentally ill, or did a household member attempt suicide?**
   Yes / No If yes, enter 1 _____

10. **Did a household member go to prison?**
Yes / No If yes, enter 1 _____

Now add your "Yes" answers: _____ **This is your ACE Score.**

Answer these two questions in a notebook or journal. After taking the ACE, we found that these questions have proven to be very helpful, important, and healing when people take the time to answer thoughtfully.

11. Is there any additional stress, trauma, or damaging experience that has impacted you in some way?

12. Go back and look at all of your "yes" responses. Write down the impact and effects those things have had on your life at the time, years, and decades later.

UNDERSTANDING YOUR ACE SCORE

You may wonder what it all means now that you've taken the ACE Assessment and have your ACE score. What does a score of 2, 4, or even 8 mean for your life, health, and path to healing? Understanding your ACE score is the next critical step toward enlightenment through self-awareness and self-acceptance. In this chapter, we'll break down the different ACE scores, explain what they reveal about the impact of your childhood experiences, and how these scores can guide you in your trauma-healing journey.

It's important to remember that your ACE score is not a life sentence. While the score reflects the adversity you've faced, it doesn't define you or determine your future. Instead, it serves as a tool for awareness, helping you identify areas of your life where trauma may have influenced your behavior, emotions, and even your health.

With awareness of your ACE Score and categories of ACEs you experienced (since each requires a different approach), you can begin to take steps toward healing, self-compassion, and personal growth.

THE RANGE OF ACE SCORES

The ACE Assessment includes ten categories of trauma. For every type of adversity you experienced in childhood, you add one point to your ACE score. The total score can range from 0 (meaning you experienced none of the listed traumas) to 10 (meaning you experienced all of the listed traumas).

Your ACE score doesn't predict your future with certainty, but it does offer insight into the risks and challenges you may face as a result of childhood trauma. Understanding the meaning behind different score ranges can provide valuable context as you progress in your healing process.

ACE Score of 0–1: Low Adversity

An ACE score of 0 or 1 means you reported experiencing relatively few of the specific types of adversity measured by the ACE Study. However, it's important to note that even a single traumatic experience, such as abuse or severe neglect, can have profound and lasting impacts on a person's life, particularly if it occurred during critical developmental periods.

What this means for you:

If you have an ACE score of 0-1, your current challenges, whether related to mental or physical health, may stem from various factors, including:

- Current life stresses
- Genetic predispositions (including epigenetics, where environmental factors can influence how your genes are expressed, potentially affecting how trauma impacts you and future generations)
- Past traumatic experiences, including those from childhood that may have been severe but singular
- Other challenging experiences not captured by the ACE questionnaire

Your score may also reflect protective factors that were present in your life, such as stable relationships, support systems, or positive role models, which could have helped buffer you from additional adversities.

Even with an ACE score of 0-1, it's crucial to honor the impact of any trauma you experienced and reflect on how specific challenges have shaped your life. Consider whether certain patterns in your life might connect to childhood experiences that the standard ACE Assessment doesn't measure. This is why I've included the extended assessment (questions 11 and 12) in this book - to help you explore these additional dimensions. Remember, healing is deeply personal, and your journey is unique, regardless of your ACE score.

ACE Score of 2–3: Moderate Adversity

An ACE score of 2 or 3 suggests you faced moderate adversity in childhood. You may have encountered difficult experiences like emotional neglect, family dysfunction, or instances of abuse. While these experiences might not have been pervasive throughout your childhood, they were significant enough to leave lasting impressions on your emotional, mental, and physical well-being.

What this means for you:

A moderate ACE score means you may be at an increased risk for some of the challenges associated with trauma, such as anxiety, depression, or difficulty in relationships. However, these risks are not deterministic. You might have also had protective factors. Perhaps a strong bond with a parent, a supportive teacher, or a stable home environment during specific periods, which helped offset some of the adverse effects of trauma.

If you find that specific patterns in your life, like self-doubt, struggles with self-worth, or trust issues are linked to these childhood experiences, developing awareness of these connections can be the first step toward healing. It is crucial to recognize, treat, and get clinically proven support and treatment solutions to help you resolve your past, present and future adverse life experiences, and integrate your improvements into your healing process so you can reduce the impact of these experiences without letting them define who you are.

ACE Score of 4–6: High Adversity

An ACE score of 4 to 6 indicates significant exposure to childhood adversity. At this level, the likelihood of experiencing long-term effects from trauma increases. Individuals with ACE scores in this range often face multiple forms of abuse, neglect, or household dysfunction. These experiences likely shaped many aspects of their development, from their emotional responses to stress to their sense of self-worth and physical health.

What this means for you:

If you have a higher ACE score, you may be at greater risk for health issues such as chronic disease, mental health challenges like PTSD, depression, or anxiety, and struggles with emotional regulation. Studies have shown that individuals with ACE scores of 4 or higher are also more likely to experience difficulties in relationships and may be more susceptible to addiction, self-harm, or other maladaptive coping mechanisms.

While these risks are real, they are not inevitable. High ACE scores reflect the challenges you've faced but highlight your strength and resilience in surviving these experiences. Understanding that it's possible to heal and lead a fulfilling, healthy life with awareness, support, and therapeutic interventions is crucial. By recognizing the impact of your childhood trauma, you can begin to take proactive steps toward healing and self-acceptance.

ACE Score of 7–10: Severe Adversity

An ACE score of 7 or higher indicates that you experienced severe and prolonged trauma during your childhood. Individuals with scores in this range often grew up in environments where multiple forms of abuse, neglect, and dysfunction were present, creating a constant state of stress and instability. The likelihood of experiencing significant health, emotional, and relational difficulties later in life is heightened with such a score.

What this means for you:

For individuals with severe ACE scores, the long-term effects of childhood trauma can be profound. Research shows that those with ACE scores of 7 or higher have a much higher risk of developing chronic health conditions such as heart disease, diabetes, or cancer. Mental health struggles, including severe depression, anxiety, and complex PTSD, are also more common. These individuals may have grown up in environments where survival was the primary focus.

Despite these challenges, an important message remains: trauma is not destiny. Your ACE score reflects what happened to you but does not define who you are or your healing capacity. Many people with high ACE scores lead meaningful, healthy lives through self-awareness, self-acceptance, resolving the root causes, and a variety of therapies, healing arts, and support systems. The healing journey may require more profound work, but the reward is a greater sense of self-understanding, compassion, and empowerment. This book is your perfect counterpart for the journey!

Awareness of your ACEs with the right help leads to acceptance, which leads to letting go and releasing emotionally, mentally, and physically. This includes finishing unfinished inner struggles with the cooperation of your Inner Critic, which we'll explore later in this book.

THE IMPACT OF ACE SCORES ON HEALTH AND WELL-BEING

The ACE Study revealed a clear connection between higher ACE scores and increased risks for various health and behavioral issues. The higher your ACE score, the more likely you will experience specific negative outcomes. Yet majority of traumas, ACEs, tragedies, and pains in most people are left untreated and unresolved. These can include:

- **Physical Health Risks:**
  Higher ACE scores are associated with an increased likelihood of developing chronic illnesses such as heart disease, cardiovascular disease, autoimmune challenges, diabetes, liver disease, and obesity. This is mainly due to the way chronic stress, caused by trauma, affects the body's systems over time.

- **Mental Health Challenges:**
  Trauma survivors with high ACE scores often struggle with mental health issues like depression, anxiety, PTSD, substance abuse, and addiction. Because they haven't connected their ACEs with their challenges, many people never realize that their dependency/addiction began around the same time as their traumatic event. These emotional challenges are a direct result of the ways childhood trauma shapes brain development and stress responses. Without proper treatment, these mental health issues not only go unresolved but may worsen over time.

- **Behavioral and Relational Difficulties:**
  High ACE scores can lead to difficulties in maintaining healthy relationships. You may struggle with trust, boundaries, and emotional regulation, all of which stem from unresolved childhood trauma. Additionally, individuals with higher ACE scores are more likely to engage in risky behaviors such as substance abuse or self-harm as a way of coping with unresolved pain.

RESILIENCE AND HEALING: YOUR ACE SCORE IS NOT THE WHOLE STORY

While the ACE Assessment helps identify the risks associated with childhood trauma, it's crucial to remember that it doesn't account for resilience. Resilience factors like supportive relationships, positive environments, the development of coping skills, and access to personalized clinically proven treatment solutions play a significant role in mitigating the effects of trauma. These protective factors can drastically reduce the impact of even the most severe ACE scores.

Your ACE score is a guide, not a verdict. It helps you understand the depth and scope of your past experiences, but your ongoing choices, healing practices, and support systems determine your future. Healing is possible at any ACE score, and awareness is always the first step.

CHAPTER 3

THE POWER OF POSITIVE CHILDHOOD EXPERIENCES (PCE)

While the ACE (Adverse Childhood Experiences) Study highlights the profound impact of trauma, it is equally important to acknowledge that childhood isn't only shaped by adversity. Despite difficult and traumatic experiences, many of us had moments of safety, connection, and joy that offered resilience and hope. These Positive Childhood Experiences (PCEs) are as critical to understanding our healing journey as our ACEs.

In this chapter, we'll explore the PCE (Positive Childhood Experiences) assessment, why it's vital to give credit to the positive aspects of our childhood, and how these experiences can help offset the damage caused by trauma. By recognizing the strengths and support we received as children, we can expand our awareness, deepen our understanding of how resilience is built, and appreciate how these positive factors play a crucial role in healing from trauma.

SHIFTING THE FOCUS: FROM TRAUMA TO RESILIENCE

The trauma-informed approach brought to prominence through the ACE Study, has helped millions of people gain a clearer understanding of how their early life experiences affect their mental, emotional, and physical health. But focusing solely on adversity doesn't tell the whole story of who we are. Resilience, which is the capacity to recover and thrive despite challenges, often comes from positive experiences that are equally influential in shaping who we become.

For many, the presence of loving relationships, safe environments, and nurturing experiences provided crucial protective factors against the impact of trauma. These positive influences don't erase the harm caused by adverse experiences, but they offer balance, showing us that we are more than just the sum of our trauma. Recognizing and celebrating the positive aspects of your childhood is an essential part of healing because it helps you see yourself not only as a survivor of adversity but as someone who also had moments of love, joy, and safety.

CHAPTER 3

WHAT IS THE PCE ASSESSMENT?

The Positive Childhood Experiences (PCE) assessment is a relatively new tool designed to measure the presence of critical positive experiences during childhood. The assessment focuses on factors that promote resilience and emotional well-being, especially in adversity. It highlights the importance of supportive relationships, emotional safety, and opportunities for personal growth, all of which help children develop a sense of worth, belonging and the ability to overcome difficulties.

The PCE assessment consists of seven key questions that explore various aspects of positive childhood experiences. These questions are focused on whether, during childhood, you experienced:

1 **Feeling Able to Talk to Family About Feelings:**
   Did you feel you could openly discuss your feelings with at least one family member? Emotional expression and validation within the family environment are vital for developing emotional intelligence and a healthy sense of self-worth.

2 **Feeling Supported by Family in Times of Crisis:**
   Did your family provide support and protection during times of stress or crisis? This sense of safety can mitigate the effects of trauma and teach you that you are worthy of care and protection.

3 **Feeling Safe and Protected at Home:**
   Did you feel physically and emotionally safe in your home environment? Consistent safety is foundational to mental health and provides the stability to cope with adversity.

4 **Enjoying Participation in Community Traditions:**
   Did you have the opportunity to engage in community or cultural traditions? These experiences help foster a sense of belonging and connection to a more significant social identity, strengthening resilience.

5 **Feeling Supported by Friends:**
   Did you have friends or peers who supported you and with whom you could share experiences? Healthy social relationships outside the family are crucial for emotional development and resilience.

6 **Having at Least Two Non-Parent Adults Who Took a Genuine Interest in You:**
   Were there any adults (such as teachers, coaches, or relatives) outside your immediate family who cared about your well-being and supported your growth? Positive adult role models provide guidance and validation, especially when parental figures may not have been reliable sources of support.

7 **Feeling a Sense of Belonging in School:**
   Did you feel connected to your school and sense that your teachers cared about you? A positive school environment can be a refuge for children experiencing stress at home, providing structure, encouragement, and social opportunities.

Each "yes" response to these questions reflects a positive experience that likely contributed to your resilience. Like the ACE score, the PCE score helps paint a complete picture of your childhood. However, instead of focusing solely on adversity, it sheds light on the moments of care, safety, and support that may have bolstered your ability to cope with difficult circumstances.

WHY POSITIVE CHILDHOOD EXPERIENCES MATTER

Acknowledging your Positive Childhood Experiences is not about minimizing or erasing your trauma. Instead, it's about recognizing the full spectrum of your childhood and understanding how even small, positive experiences can contribute to resilience and healing. Here's why PCEs are a vital part of the trauma-healing process:

1. They Build Resilience
Research has shown that children who experience positive, supportive relation-

ships and environments are more likely to develop the emotional and psychological resilience needed to navigate adversity. These positive experiences lay the groundwork for healthy self-esteem, emotional regulation, and the ability to form meaningful relationships in adulthood.

Understanding that positive childhood experiences played a role in building their resilience can be empowering. It reinforces the idea that even in the face of hardship, you were capable of receiving and giving love, forming bonds, and finding joy. This realization helps expand your sense of self beyond the role of "victim" toward an identity rooted in strength and wholeness.

2. They Offer Emotional Safety
Positive childhood experiences, whether from family, friends, or the community, offered a sense of safety and validation. This emotional safety is crucial for healing because it provides a counterbalance to the feelings of fear, shame, or unworthiness that often arise from trauma. By remembering and acknowledging these safe moments, you can access the emotional resources to confront and process painful memories.

3. They Provide a Model for Healthy Relationships
PCEs often involve relationships with caring adults, peers, or mentors who provide support and guidance. These relationships serve as a model for what healthy, loving connections look like. For those who experienced dysfunctional or abusive relationships as children, these positive examples can be invaluable in helping to form healthier connections in adulthood.

By reflecting on the positive relationships you had as a child, you can begin to build on those experiences in your current life. Whether cultivating more supportive friendships, seeking out mentors, or strengthening family bonds, these early experiences provide a blueprint for creating healthy relationships in the present.

4. They Help Offset the Damage of ACEs
One of the most critical findings in recent trauma research is that positive childhood experiences can offset some of the adverse effects of ACEs with positive

role-modeling, caring relationships and compassionate support. While adversity in childhood increases the risk of physical and mental health issues, positive experiences can reduce these risks by providing a buffer against the harmful effects of trauma.

For instance, research has shown that individuals with high PCE scores are more likely to report good mental health and lower levels of depression and anxiety, even if they have high ACE scores. The presence of supportive relationships, safe environments, and growth opportunities can help mitigate the long-term damage of adversity, giving survivors a better chance at healing and thriving.

5. They Foster Hope and Gratitude
Recognizing the positive aspects of your childhood fosters a sense of gratitude and hope. Trauma can sometimes cloud our memories, making it difficult to see the good amidst the pain. By intentionally reflecting on moments of love, joy, or support, you can shift your focus from what was lost or broken to what was gained and built. This shift doesn't ignore the pain but adds balance, reminding you that even in the most challenging times, there were glimmers of light.

THE IMPORTANCE OF PCES IN THE HEALING PROCESS

Awareness with acceptance and support are the foundation of healing, which means becoming aware of both the challenges and the gifts of your past. The PCE assessment allows you to see that, even if you endured significant trauma, there were also moments of care, connection, and joy that helped shape who you are today. By acknowledging these experiences, you can begin to integrate the positive aspects of your childhood into your healing journey.

Here is why the PCE assessment is so important to this step of awareness with acceptance and support:

- **It Provides a Fuller Picture of Your Childhood:**
  The ACE Assessment clearly explains the challenges you faced, but the PCE assessment offers a balanced perspective, showing you the sources of strength

and resilience that were also present. This fuller picture allows for more compassionate self-awareness.

- **It Helps You Acknowledge What's Right About Your Life, the Good:**
  Many trauma survivors are so focused on the negative experiences of their childhood that they forget to acknowledge the positive. The PCE assessment encourages you to take stock of the good in your life, both then and now, creating space for gratitude and healing.

- **It Highlights Your Capacity for (Deep) Healing:**
  Recognizing that you had positive, supportive experiences, even amid adversity, can remind you of your inner strength and capacity for healing. It reinforces the idea that you are not defined solely by your trauma but also by your resilience.

  It Informs Your Healing Path:
- Understanding your PCEs can help you identify the relationships, activities, or practices that have historically been sources of strength for you. These positive experiences can inform the healing practices you engage in today, helping you cultivate more of what worked for you in the past.

MOVING FORWARD: INTEGRATING THE POSITIVE WITH THE PAIN

Healing from trauma is not just about confronting and resolving the pain of the past; it's also about recognizing the moments of joy, love, and support that were part of your story. The PCE assessment offers a way to balance your understanding of your childhood, helping you see that despite adversity, there were bright spots that helped you survive and grow.

As you progress in your healing journey, allow these positive memories and experiences to guide you. Use them as a source of strength, a reminder of your resilience, and a foundation to build a more compassionate, self-accepting future. In the next chapter, we will explore how to begin integrating this awareness of both the ACEs and PCEs into practical steps for healing and self-acceptance. You can create a path toward wholeness and true self-compassion by honoring both the pain and the positive.

THE PCE ASSESSMENT

Prior to your 18th birthday:

> **1** **Did a parent or other adult in the household often or very often Support, compliment, encourage, or show interest in your thoughts or concerns?**
>
> Yes / No If yes, enter 1 _____
>
> **2** **Did a parent or other adult in the household often or very often hug, hold, read to you, or spend meaningful time with you?**
>
> Yes / No If yes, enter 1 _____
>
> **3** **Did an adult or someone at least five years older than you ever care for you, babysit, or tutor you in a kind and compassionate way while growing up?**
>
> Yes / No If yes, enter 1 _____
>
> **4** **Did you often or very often feel that someone in your household loved you or thought you were important or special, or did your family look out for each other, feel close, and support each other?**
>
> Yes / No If yes, enter 1 _____
>
> **5** **Did you often or very often feel that you had enough to eat and clean clothes and had someone to protect you?**
>
> Yes / No If yes, enter 1 _____
>
> **6** **Did your parents commonly show love or affection toward each other or support, compliment, or hug each other in front of you?**
>
> Yes / No If yes, enter 1 _____

7 **Did your mother or stepmother often or very often support or compliment you or kiss or hug in front of you?**

Yes / No If yes, enter 1 _____

8 **Did you live with anyone who had a good sense of humor or was musical or artistic in any way?**

Yes / No If yes, enter 1 _____

9 **Did a household member treat or communicate with your friends in a kind way?**

Yes / No If yes, enter 1 _____

10 **Did a household member study new subjects, attend college, donate time to the community, or participate in fundraisers?**

Yes / No If yes, enter 1 _____

Now add your "1" or "Yes" answers: ___ This is your PCE Score.

Answer the following two questions in a notebook or journal.

After taking the PCE, I found that these questions have proven to be very helpful, important, and healing when people take the time to answer thoughtfully.

11 Are there any additional positive experiences that have impacted you in some way? If so, please note them here.

12 Please review all your "yes" responses and write down the impact and effects each of those things have had on your life.

UNDERSTANDING YOUR PCE SCORE

Now that you've taken the Positive Childhood Experiences (PCE) Assessment and have your PCE score, it's time to explore what it all means. How do positive experiences in childhood counterbalance adversity? What can your PCE score reveal about your resilience and ability to heal from trauma? This chapter will help you understand your PCE score and how it plays a crucial role in your trauma-healing journey by acknowledging the strengths and protective factors that supported you during childhood.

Just as your ACE score highlights the impact of adversity, your PCE score highlights the supportive, nurturing experiences that helped you build resilience. A high ACE score might indicate trauma, but a high PCE score reflects the positive relationships and environments that bolstered your emotional well-being. Understanding your PCE score is essential because it provides insight into the positive forces in your life that can help you on the path toward healing and unconditional self-acceptance.

THE RANGE OF PCE SCORES

The PCE Assessment score ranges from 0 to 10, with each "yes" answer counting as "1". Each point represents a positive experience that contributed to your emotional strength and resilience. Whether you had just one positive experience or many, each one matters and can significantly influence your capacity for healing from trauma.

Your PCE score is an essential complement to your ACE score. While it doesn't erase the effects of trauma, it highlights your ability to build resilience and thrive despite it. Let's break down the different PCE score ranges and what they reveal about your past, healing journey, and resilience.

PCE Score of 0–2: Few Varied Positive Experiences
A PCE score of 0–2 indicates you experienced few of the different types of protective factors measured during childhood. While you may have had one consistent positive factor (like a supportive teacher or safe place to spend time), the overall range of protective experiences appears to have been limited. This

could mean that alongside any adversity you faced, you had reduced access to the variety of emotional support systems and safe environments that help foster resilience. It's possible you had limited people you could rely on or missed out on diverse positive experiences in your home or community.

What this means for you: If your PCE score is low, this may indicate that your trauma healing journey could feel more challenging, as you may not have had access to a wide range of protective experiences to buffer the effects of adversity. You may also find that feelings of isolation, insecurity, or mistrust stem from a lack of varied early nurturing and support. However, it's important to remember that healing is always possible, regardless of your score.

If you've had limited types of positive experiences in childhood, your healing process may involve intentionally seeking out and creating the diverse support systems and nurturing environments you lacked as a child. Surrounding yourself with safe, loving relationships now can help foster resilience that may not have fully developed in your early years.

PCE Score of 3 - 5: A Number of Positive Experiences

A PCE score of 3 to 5 suggests that you had a few positive experiences that helped foster resilience during childhood. While you may have faced challenges or adversity, some people or environments supported and nurtured your well-being, even if inconsistently. These experiences, such as having at least one trusted adult or feeling safe at school, likely helped you cope with stress and trauma to some extent.

What this means for you: With this PCE score, you may have some resilience that has helped you navigate life's challenges, though you might still struggle with lingering effects from childhood trauma. You might notice that while you are capable of forming meaningful relationships or managing stress, there are times when unresolved trauma surfaces, making you feel vulnerable or reactive. The key to healing with this PCE score is to build on the strengths you already possess. Reflect on those moments of safety, connection, and support from your childhood, and consider how they shaped your capacity to overcome adversity.

By identifying these strengths, you can leverage them as you continue your healing journey, allowing them to serve as a foundation for building self-acceptance and resilience.

PCE Score of 6 - 8: Strong Positive Experiences
A PCE score of 6 to 8 suggests that you had many positive experiences during childhood. While you may have faced challenges or adverse experiences, you also had access to substantial protective factors, such as supportive family members, trusted adults, or safe and positive environments like school or community groups. These experiences likely helped buffer the adverse effects of trauma and provided a sense of stability and belonging.

What this means for you: With a higher PCE score, you likely have a solid foundation of resilience. You may find that, despite any trauma you experienced, you can maintain healthy relationships, regulate your emotions, and cope with stress in a relatively balanced way. Your positive experiences as a child helped instill in you a sense of self-worth and security, which can be incredibly valuable on your healing journey.

However, it's essential to acknowledge that even with a strong PCE score, the effects of trauma may still be present. Your positive experiences likely helped you navigate adversity but may not have completely shielded you from its long-term impact. Healing from trauma is still necessary, but with a high PCE score, you have the advantage of a well-developed emotional toolkit to support your process.

PCE Score of 9 - 10: Highly Nurturing Childhood
A PCE score of 6 or 7 indicates that you had a profoundly nurturing childhood, with many positive experiences that fostered a strong sense of resilience, self-worth, and emotional well-being. You likely had multiple supportive relationships, felt safe and protected in your environments, and experienced a sense of belonging in your family, school, or community. These factors have given you a significant advantage in coping with adversity.

What this means for you: If you have a high PCE score, you will likely have a robust sense of resilience, which has helped you survive and thrive in the face of life's challenges. The positive experiences you had in childhood have given you a solid foundation for emotional health, enabling you to form healthy relationships, navigate stress effectively, and maintain a positive sense of self-worth.

However, even with a high PCE score, it's still important to acknowledge any trauma you may have experienced. While your resilience is a powerful asset, healing from trauma requires addressing the wounds that may still be present, even if they are less noticeable. Your high PCE score can act as a guide, showing you the strengths you already possess as you work through your trauma-healing journey.

THE IMPACT OF PCE SCORES ON HEALING AND RESILIENCE

Understanding your PCE score offers valuable insights into the protective factors that have supported you. Just as a high ACE score highlights the root of the challenges you may face, a high PCE score demonstrates your strengths. Research has shown that positive childhood experiences can help offset the adverse effects of ACEs, making your PCE score a crucial piece of your healing journey.

PCES AND EMOTIONAL RESILIENCE

Positive childhood experiences help foster emotional resilience, which is the ability to bounce back from adversity. If you had supportive relationships, felt safe in your home or school, and had opportunities to express your feelings, you likely developed emotional tools that helped you cope with stress and trauma. Emotional regulation, self-compassion, and the ability to seek help are essential for healing and personal growth.

PCES AND RELATIONAL HEALTH

In childhood, positive relationships with family members, friends, or other adults teach you how to form healthy, trusting connections with others. A high PCE score reflects a childhood where you were able to experience safe, supportive relationships, which can be a significant advantage in adult life. This relational health is crucial for healing from trauma, as it allows you to seek out and maintain the supportive connections you need to heal and thrive.

PCES AS A BUFFER AGAINST TRAUMA

One of the most significant findings in recent trauma research is that positive childhood experiences can act as a buffer against the long-term effects of ACEs. Even if you have a high ACE score, a strong PCE score can help reduce your risk for mental health challenges, chronic illness, and relational difficulties. Your positive experiences help create a foundation of resilience, enabling you to recover from trauma more effectively.

MOVING FORWARD WITH YOUR PCE SCORE

Now that you understand your PCE score, you can use this awareness to inform your healing process. Reflect on the positive experiences from your childhood and consider how they shaped your ability to cope with adversity. These experiences are a powerful resource in your journey toward self-acceptance, reminding you that you are not defined solely by your trauma but also by your capacity for resilience and growth.

Your ACE and PCE scores help provide a comprehensive understanding of your past. By recognizing the interplay between adversity and resilience, you can move forward with greater self-awareness, compassion, and hope for healing.

Next, I will share my favorite technique for aiding you on this first step from trauma to enlightenment: Awareness. This solution has helped thousands heal trauma and lead happy, empowered, and vibrant lives.

CHAPTER 4

AN EXERCISE TO EMPOWER SELF-ACCEPTANCE, SELF-UNDERSTANDING, SELF-ADVOCACY AND INCREASED SELF-AWARENESS

Now that you are more aware of your ACEs and PCEs, it's time to examine your life story and consider how certain experiences shaped who you are and how you think today.

Difficult life experiences, including loss, stress and trauma can drive thoughts and behaviors without us even being aware of them. By reflecting on our past beyond judgment, we can unearth our inner wisdom, our authentic present self, and bring these traumas to the light (our consciousness) to heal them gently, effectively, and compassionately.

To aid you in this process of awareness, I'd like to share one of my most effective ACE Treatment solutions: "Going to the Movies."

GOING TO THE MOVIES

Start by imagining a movie theater. Visualize, picture, feel, remember, smell and enjoy all of the theater details. Sense the smell of popcorn, visualize the red velvet curtains, the dim lighting, feel the comfortable seats. Maybe it's an IMAX theater or one with reclining seats! You enter the theater, choose your seat, get settled, and the movie has already started. But this time, the movie on the big screen is all about you and your life from your very beginning right up to the present. Soon, you will also be watching the movie of your life as it unfolds and blossoms into your future.

You are the star, the main character, and it's your story, past to present. It's your work life, home life, performance, and how you deal with people, demands, success, and failure. It's a movie about your whole life.

This movie includes everything, from your sweetest, most beautiful memories to challenging traumas. Perhaps you can even begin to witness some patterns you've picked up from your ACEs and PCEs.

When you are sitting in the 15th row—right in the middle of the theater—you are embodying your Inner Critic. This is the judgmental, controlling, never-satisfied part of you. We all have this Inner Critic watching our movie, ready to tell us everything that's wrong with us.

This critic tells you everything you did wrong, could have done differently, or didn't do but "should've." Your Inner Critic loves the word "should"!

This is your perfectionist, too.

But there's another "you" in the theater, too, sitting quietly in the very last row of the theater: your Last Row Self. Your Last Row Self is your inner wisdom, creativity, peace of mind, relaxed, compassionate, inner doctor as well as the part of you that understands the importance of your freedom. It's the "you" when you feel calm and peaceful, and where you can observe and listen to your movie and your Inner Critic in the 15th row with friendliness, care, compassion, understanding and love.

The Three Perspectives When You Go to the Movies

1. **You as the Star of the Movie:** working, playing, driving, shopping, dealing with bosses, raising kids, keeping schedules, and feeling pushed, hurried, and stressed. This is your CONSCIOUS mind.

2. **Your Inner Critic in the 15th row:** ready to find fault and punish you for your mistakes. The part of you that gets stuck in stress. This is your SUBCONSCIOUS mind.

3. **The Last Row:** the friendly, caring, and compassionate part of you that loves yourself just as you are, including your Inner Critic. This is your UNCONSCIOUS mind.

CHAPTER 4

GOING TO THE MOVIES IN THREE STEPS

Now that you know the concept of "Going to the Movies" and can visualize your inner theater, it's time to practice. To raise awareness around your past stress, difficulties, traumas, positive experiences, and current challenges, do these three steps, in order: In the future, as you develop your capacity to be flexible, helpful, proactive and self-accepting, you will be able to shift your consciousness with ease between your conscious, subconscious and unconscious, or your movie, your 15th row and your last row.

Step 1
Be in your movie. Be present in the moment and experience what's happening in your movie. Let the scene unfold; feel yourself acting your role. Let yourself be present with, express, and feel whatever you feel in that scene. Become aware of what comes up for you when you reenact scenes of the past. Focus on what's happening in your movie. Specifically, what's going on emotionally, physically and in your relationships. These three mirror one another. If you are tense physically, you are tense emotionally and you are tense in your relationships. The opposite is also true. When you are relaxed about your relationship, you are relaxed emotionally and relaxed in your body. Also, how you are during your waking hours is how you are in your sleeping hours; tense or relaxed. Just as the last thing you think and feel when you are going to sleep is always the first thing you think and feel when you are waking up.

Step 2
Now, move your awareness to the 15th row. Let your Inner Critic criticize the scenes, you, your body, your feelings, your relationships and your life. From the 15th row, focus on what's wrong with you and your thoughts and feelings. Let your Inner Critic express its opinions about what happened or didn't. Let your Inner Critic be hostile and have its say. While difficult, it's important to become aware and express the feelings you still carry when you think of certain things of the past so that you can begin to heal moving forward. Even simply bringing certain things into the light can release their grip. This is a breakthrough opportunity because you are no longer fighting this part of you or trying to get rid of it, which just makes it stronger, never works and is a waste of time, and energy. You

will be learning how to communicate and support this well-trained part of you, so it becomes a bridge to your last row and not a wall.

Step 3

Imagine getting up and walking back to the last row of the theater. Visualize yourself getting up and physically moving. In the last row, watch your movie and your 15th row Inner Critic with detachment, connection, compassion, and understanding. Sometimes, you may even see the absurdity and discover your sense of humor. Become aware and accept your breathing as it is. As you are learning how to accept yourself as you are, as you are developing your capacity to accept your movie (feelings, body and relationships) to help transport yourself to your last-row perspective to feel freer, calmer, more peaceful, relaxed, observing, and comfortable with yourself while feeling more friendly, caring, and compassionate.

Keep coming back to this technique. Going to the last row is coming home to YOU, the genuine, authentic you that doesn't carry around unnecessary stress, old, unwanted shame, and an abundance of self-criticism. The more you practice, the more you will live with the last-row perspective with patience, purpose and TLC, and be able to move back there whenever needed.

STUCK WITH YOUR CRITIC

It's not always easy to move to the last row because, to do so, you must spend some time listening to your pesky Inner Critic in the 15th row. In my experience, most people try to eliminate their Inner Critic. They do years of therapy, go to seminars, read books, and take medications—all to get rid of their Inner Critic.

But it isn't possible. Why? Because your Inner Critic is a part of you, whether you like it or not!

Your Inner Critic is part of your internal programming, and it's too much a part of your life to be silenced or eliminated. It's created by all the internal and external criticisms you've experienced for a lifetime, and you've strengthened it by resisting it for all these years. So, don't waste your time thinking you will eliminate the 15th-row Inner Critic. It has a lifetime membership.

Instead of fighting your Inner Critic and getting stuck in the 15th row, just accept your Inner Critic, breathe, and walk back to the last row. You can accept that your 15th row Inner Critic is part of you and has a voice but from the last row. With friendliness, caring, and compassion, you will understand that your Inner Critic is trying in its negative way to help you.

Remember, once in a while your Inner Critic is correct. Has it ever told you someone or a situation wasn't good for you, and it was right?

So, if it's correct 10% of the time, that helps.

The other 90%, listen, say "thank you for trying to help me," and then accept, express and let go to get to your last row.

The last row perspective is free from old guilt, old stress, other's judgment and past traumas. It focuses on what's right about you and empathizes with your humanness. Moving to the last row allows you to gently bring awareness to your life story, stress, life lessons, personal improvement, traumas, and their effects on you so you can take the first step from trauma to enlightenment.

As you practice this technique in everyday life, always finish in your last row perspective.

TIPS FOR GOING TO THE MOVIES

This technique is excellent for becoming aware of your stress, difficulties, pains, traumas and the psychological hold they may still have on you. It's also beneficial if you become triggered or experience stress in the present moment.

Here are a few tips that will make this technique successful in those moments:

- **Try to do it as close to your moment of stress as possible.** The sooner you respond to your stress, the sooner you will relax, feel the shift to the last row, and find yourself again.

- **If you have to wait, don't put it off too long.** Try to complete the process that same day or night.

- **Take your time and proceed at your own pace.** Your practice time will change as you learn the process. At first, you might spend 50 minutes to an hour in your inner theater. With more practice, five to 10 minutes a day may be just right. Soon it will become second nature, virtually automatic, and you will be practicing more on an as-needed basis.

- **The time you spend on different steps will vary every day.** One day you might need more time on screen and less time with your 15th Row Inner Critic. Just stay sensitive and flexible to your needs, and always finish in the last row.

- **Results will vary, so be patient.** In the Last Row, new, creative solutions may surprise you, bubbling up in just a few seconds. At other times, it might take a few minutes, hours or days in the Last Row before you feel the shift to positive, individualized resolutions. Be patient: Patience is a sign of inner and calm power.

- **Once in the Last Row, prepare to see your life from a whole new perspective.** Your moments of stress will seem small and unimportant, and you'll feel relaxed and renewed.

- **Always finish in the Last Row.** This is the place of ultimate protection in your life. There's nobody to bother you, no one to disturb you and no one else to take care of. You can take the best possible care of yourself in the last row, and everyone else you care about can come right after that.

PART TWO: UNDERSTANDING

CHAPTER 5
TRANSLATING AWARENESS INTO UNDERSTANDING

Awareness is the spark that begins your journey from trauma to enlightenment. When you recognize the patterns and emotional imprints left by trauma, you ignite a vital sense of self-awareness. But awareness alone, without action or reflection, risks becoming stagnant. The next crucial step on this path is understanding, which is an active, compassionate exploration that turns awareness into a bridge toward healing.

THE BRIDGE BETWEEN AWARENESS AND UNDERSTANDING

Understanding is the phase where insight takes shape. If awareness is a light illuminating the room of your mind, understanding is your decision to step into that room, inspect its corners, and rearrange its contents. It is a deeper engagement with your inner world, inviting you to notice what is there and comprehend its meaning.

But how do you move from simply being aware to truly understanding? This chapter will guide you through translating your awareness into meaningful insights that propel you forward. It begins by interpreting what you discovered while Going to the Movies and your ACE and PCE assessment results. Essentially, we are turning your awareness into wisdom.

Step One: Reflecting on Your Movie and Assessments

If you've taken the time to evaluate the behaviors, triggers, and emotional responses you had in the past when watching the movie of your life, you now hold valuable information. This is especially true after taking the ACE and PCE, which gave you useful insights into where these behaviors may have originated. Each insight is a piece of your puzzle, revealing clues about how trauma has shaped your thoughts, beliefs, and reactions.

Reflect on your Going to the Movies exercise in the last chapter with an open mind. Ask yourself:

- Which areas of my life feel the most impacted by past trauma?
- What beliefs or recurring patterns did I identify while "Going to the Movies?"
- How do these patterns manifest in my relationships, work, or self-perception?

Write these observations down, but don't rush through them. Understanding begins when you slow down and look beyond the surface. If the exercise revealed, for example, that you often feel anxious in social settings, explore why. What stories do you tell yourself when anxiety arises? What past experiences reinforce these feelings? This reflective practice helps lay the groundwork for more profound insight.

Step Two: Looking for Patterns and Connections

As you delve into your observations, you will begin to notice patterns. These patterns are essential to understanding the way trauma has influenced your psyche. Identifying them helps you recognize that what might initially seem like isolated behaviors or reactions are interconnected.

For instance, if your movie showed your tendency to avoid conflict at all costs, trace this habit back. Did you grow up in an environment where expressing anger was unsafe? Did you learn to prioritize peace over authenticity as a survival mechanism? Recognizing such connections is a powerful moment on the path to enlightenment. It helps shift self-blame into self-compassion. It encourages you to see that many of your reactions were adaptive responses to challenging experiences.

Step Three: The Importance of Context

Understanding must always be contextual. Trauma leaves imprints on the mind that are highly individual, shaped by circumstances unique to each person. To move beyond surface awareness, consider the context in which your patterns developed. Ask yourself:

- What were the conditions surrounding the formation of these beliefs?
- Were there external pressures, relationships, or environments that reinforced them?

The goal is not to dwell on the past or assign blame but to understand how and why your mind created these coping mechanisms. This insight makes it easier to break free from outdated narratives and transform them into conscious choices that align with your current self.

Step Four: Transforming Insight into Understanding

The true essence of understanding is to extract wisdom from your reflections. Begin to shift your perspective from What happened to me? to What did I learn from what happened? and How can this understanding serve me now?

A significant part of this step is realizing that your past coping mechanisms, though they may feel restrictive now, were once strategies for survival. Appreciating this fact softens self-judgment and builds a foundation for forgiveness, both for yourself and for others, when applicable.

With understanding, you can start to see the choices before you. Your trauma no longer solely defines you but instead informs you. This realization allows you to cultivate new responses that align with the life you wish to create, paving the way for deeper healing.

Integrating Understanding into Daily Life

Finally, understanding is most effective when it becomes part of your daily existence. Practice incorporating these insights by:

- Creating authentic and personalized affirmations that challenge old beliefs ("I, (your name) am safe to be real about how I feel with myself and trustworthy people").
- Setting small, achievable goals that test new patterns ("I will advocate for myself and others that are worthy in this meeting").
- Engaging in practices that connect the mind, emotions, and body, such as listening with unconditional acceptance, breathwork, pleasant walks in nature, and grounding exercises.

Understanding is not a static destination but an ongoing process. The more you practice reflecting, contextualizing, and integrating new insights, the deeper your comprehension becomes. Each step builds resilience and empowers you to

CHAPTER 5

move forward with greater clarity and self-assurance.

This chapter marks a pivotal transition from merely being aware of your wounds to understanding their roots, meanings, and lessons. With understanding, you become equipped to navigate life and shape it, progressing from trauma to enlightenment.

CHAPTER 6
UNPACKING YOUR UNIQUE TRAUMA RESPONSES AND COPING MECHANISMS

In Part One of this book, awareness sheds light on your emotional and behavioral patterns, and in Chapter 5, your initial understanding begins to piece together the reasons behind these patterns. Now, the journey deepens as you explore how your personal interpretations of trauma, your coping mechanisms, and their origins interconnect to form your unique response to the world.

THE COMPLEXITY OF TRAUMA RESPONSES

Trauma responses are as varied as the individuals who experience them. While many people may develop similar coping mechanisms, the context and meaning behind them differ greatly from one person to the next. What may be a subtle withdrawal for one person could represent a profound act of self-preservation for another. This chapter invites you to explore your unique interpretation of these responses and how they came to be.

EXPLORING YOUR TRAUMA RESPONSES

Trauma responses often fit into four broad categories: fight, flight, freeze, and fawn (fawning is a trauma response where a person behaves in a people-pleasing way to avoid conflict and establish a sense of safety).

Each response is a learned and practiced reaction to perceived threats, but they manifest differently in each person depending on their history and environment. Reflect on the following questions as you explore your trauma responses:

- Which trauma response(s) do I identify with most? (e.g., do I often become defensive, retreat, feel paralyzed, or overly accommodating?)
- When do these responses tend to appear in my life?
- How do these responses protect me or make me feel safe?

For example, if you tend to freeze during conflict, consider how this response might have developed. Did you grow up in a chaotic or unpredictable environment where staying still and quiet was the safest choice? Or, if you lean toward a fawn response, did you learn that appeasing others minimized the potential for harm or conflict? Understanding these roots offers clarity and compassion for yourself.

THE ORIGINS OF COPING MECHANISMS

Coping mechanisms are learned behaviors and mental strategies developed to navigate stressful or traumatic experiences. These mechanisms may have served you well in the past but could now hinder growth and connection. To explore your coping mechanisms, consider:

- Which behaviors or thought patterns do I engage in when I feel threatened or anxious? (e.g., overworking, overeating, avoidance, numbing with substances or distractions)
- What are the benefits of these mechanisms, and what are the costs?

For instance, hyper-independence may have developed to avoid vulnerability if trusting others once led to disappointment or harm. While this strategy likely helped you survive and retain control in difficult times, it may isolate you from meaningful support and connection.

THE ROLE OF PERSONAL INTERPRETATION

A crucial part of exploring trauma responses is understanding how personal interpretation shapes these reactions. Your perception of an event holds more power over your response than the event itself. This is why two people exposed to similar situations may develop vastly different coping mechanisms. Your upbringing, belief system, and emotional resilience all contribute to how you process and respond to trauma.

Reflect on moments where your internal dialogue influenced your reaction:

- How do I interpret my experiences when I'm triggered or under stress? (e.g., "I'm not safe," "I can't trust anyone," "I need to be perfect to be loved")
- How have these interpretations shaped my self-concept and worldview?

Understanding your individual interpretations helps you see that trauma responses are not random or illogical but deeply tied to the stories you tell yourself. Perhaps an experience of abandonment led you to interpret later relationships with heightened suspicion. Recognizing this link allows you to rewrite these narratives with conscious effort.

IDENTIFYING HIDDEN PATTERNS AND ROOT CAUSES

To fully understand your coping mechanisms, trace them back to their origins, which could be highlighted through the ACE and PCE assessments you took earlier in this book, or when you practiced Going to the Movies.

The Going to the Movies exercise involves recognizing the early experiences that taught you to react in specific ways. You might start by identifying moments of trauma or stress and mapping how you adapted in response:

- What early experiences shaped my current coping strategies?
- How did I learn that these strategies were effective or necessary?

For example, if your coping mechanism is to constantly seek validation, look for memories that taught you approval equaled safety or love. Did you have caregivers whose attention or affection depended on your achievements or behavior? Such early conditions often embed deeply held beliefs that continue to influence adult behavior.

REFRAMING YOUR PERSPECTIVE

Understanding the origins of your trauma responses is empowering because it allows you to see your actions not as failures or flaws but as adaptive strategies that serve a purpose. This recognition brings an opportunity to reframe your self-perception with compassion:

- How can I view my past coping mechanisms through a lens of empathy rather than judgment?
- What would it look like to honor the part of me that developed these strategies and gently guide it toward healthier responses?

For instance, if you've relied on avoiding conflict to stay safe, acknowledging that this once protected you can help you appreciate your resourcefulness. From this place of understanding, you can practice new, more empowering ways of engaging with conflict that align with your current needs and values.

MOVING TOWARD HOLISTIC AND CONSCIOUS COPING

Exploring and understanding your trauma responses and their origins is the beginning of moving toward conscious coping. This means shifting from automatic, survival-based reactions to deliberate, choice-driven responses. While it takes time and practice, you can transform instinctive responses into thoughtful actions that serve your growth and well-being:

- Start with small changes, such as pausing when triggered to breathe and reflect before responding.
- Practice replacing old narratives with affirmations that support new beliefs, such as "I am safe to express my feelings" or "I am worthy of love and respect as I am."

Your trauma responses, no matter how ingrained, well-practiced, programmed, conditioned, or automatic, were born out of a need to survive. By exploring their roots and understanding how they were shaped by personal interpretation, you can make peace with them and begin to reshape your path from trauma to enlightenment with mindful intention.

CHAPTER 7
A STRATEGY TO DEVELOP A DEEPER SELF-UNDERSTANDING AND EMPATHY

The questions posed in the previous chapters are designed to help you better understand yourself and how you see and respond to the world. Please continue practicing the Going to the Movies exercise and revisit the questions posed in the previous chapters to challenge and reframe your perspective.

While working through this process with clients and patients worldwide, we've also shared some simple strategies to deepen their understanding and empathy toward themselves during this critical step.

Becoming aware of and understanding our trauma and trauma responses isn't always an easy task, so it's good to have a technique on hand to keep you grounded, present, and compassionate with yourself.

In this chapter, I'll share my Committee Meeting exercise to help you cultivate a more profound sense of understanding and empathy toward yourself as you continue on the path from trauma to enlightenment.

THE COMMITTEE MEETING STRATEGY

This exercise invites you to hold a personal "committee meeting" with your emotions—your inner committee members. Each emotion develops at different points to help you cope and protect yourself. While some were helpful in the past, they may now block your progress.

Your committee members, your emotions, were born of your different life experiences and coping skills that may have been conscious or subconscious.

When you first begin, you can understand, respect, and resolve their influence by acknowledging and giving each emotion a voice, with or without judgment. With a little bit of practice and the new skills you will learn in this chapter, you will learn how to go through this process with awareness, acceptance, expressing (letting go), and judging because these will lead you to breakthrough opportunities and, as a result, be free of judgment.

CHAPTER 7

Paradoxically and counter-intuitively, allowing yourself to judge your committee members will become a bridge instead of a wall to your judgment-free perspective.

People continually get stuck with trauma, stress, and adverse life experiences because they try their best to do the impossible: stop feeling what they genuinely feel (repress their committee members), control their feelings (committee members), and try to stop, deny, stuff, and judge their genuine feelings.

Repressing emotions only strengthens them, contributing to stress, anxiety, or depression. Instead, you will learn to work with them safely and effectively, creating space for growth and healing.

Your inner committee is unique to you, shaped by past experiences and traumas. Members like *Hurt, Afraid, Hopeful,* or *Angry* are all valid and deserve to be heard. Even challenging emotions have a purpose; when treated with care, they can help you move forward.

Through this process, your committee members will be able to communicate and coexist in harmony so you can feel free, clear, and empowered on your journey from trauma to enlightenment.

Everyone has their committee members inside. And no two people have the same inner committee. So, I'll show you exactly how to work through the entire committee meeting process and develop your own personal, satisfying, and empowering resolutions.
Let's get started.

Identifying your Committee Members
Everyone has diffrent committee members. Who is at your committee meeting table?

Here are some examples of committee members you may have:

- Worried
- I don't care
- Afraid
- Needy
- Hopeful
- Desperate
- Helpless
- Powerless
- Confident
- Happy
- Jealous
- Guilty
- Ashamed
- Frustrated
- Hopeful
- Sad
- Angry
- Lonely
- Betrayed
- Hopeful
- Fake It Till You Make It!

Here is an example to help you identify committee members:

Let's say you had a negative experience in childhood that caused the committee member "Afraid" to come about. Then, you had trouble getting along with the other kids in school. "Angry" joined the committee. As you got older, you excelled in a sport, and "Confidence" became a part of your committee. You experienced body changes in junior high, and "Awkward" and "Unsure" joined the meeting. As you moved into adulthood, you had different committee members who developed as part of your struggle to cope with the feelings from earlier stages.

Remember, one of the most important things is recognizing that nothing is wrong with any of your committee members. There is nothing that any of them did that was bad. Most likely, your committee has been struggling, fighting,

CHAPTER 7

holding back, and even acting out to cope with your trauma.

All your committee members can learn to safely express their feelings and even get along with one another. The biggest mistake people make is thinking that they can deny their feelings. When you push your feelings down, they don't disappear. Instead, your body becomes the receptacle for those repressed feelings. Have you noticed that stress can give you a stomachache, headache, or backache? Soon, you will safely and comfortably give each committee member a voice by writing their feelings down in your journal and expressing them instead of repressing them.

You'll go through your committee members, one at a time, and then resolve your whole committee meeting in a way that will help you immediately and into the future. It's incredible to think that the same committee that's challenged you all these years will help you finally feel enlightened!

Some of our patients have said that simply the awareness of their committee members made them feel better. When they learned to resolve their internal fighting, they felt incredibly free. Some people even identify their committee members as their masculine or feminine side, inner child, critical parent, or rebellious teenager.

Feel free to look at the list of possible committee members above, identify which ones are on your committee, and add any that aren't on the list. Many people like to imagine their committee sitting around a table with chairs; others want to imagine the committee meeting outside under a tree on the grass, ready to begin the process.

Prepare for the Committee Meeting

The issue they are meeting about first is how you've been coping with your trauma and whatever patterns, mechanisms, or bad habits you've developed to manage it. You will have more meetings about this, but first, you will learn how to implement the whole strategy to be successful and see results.

STEP 1: Awareness
I recommend you use a journal or a few pieces of paper the first time you do this exercise.

First, write down one coping mechanism or conflict in the middle of the paper: the one you feel ready to resolve or that's most important. Circle it.

Put the words representing how you feel about the specific challenge in a circle around that word or phrase in the center. These are your committee members who have joined the meeting to discuss this particular topic. Below this circle of words, write how you've coped. Perhaps it's food, gambling, cigarettes, alcohol, relationships, caffeine, work, shopping, power, money, exercise, success or failure, low self-esteem, or negative emotions.

When you write down your committee members, don't worry about putting them in order, priority, or intensity. The only important thing here is identifying each without getting caught in judgment.

STEP 2: Acceptance
Before any committee members express themselves, it's essential to set up safety exits and support to exit the exercise if necessary and get comfortable until you want to continue.

In your journal, describe your place of safety or comfort, where you would love to retreat in times of stress. Imagine yourself in the observer's perspective, like when you watched your movie from the last row in Part One. This time, imagine you're above the committee meeting members you've identified, looking down, always with the care, sensitivity, and understanding of the last-row observer.

STEP 3: Expressing, Communicating, and Letting Go (Giving Each of Them a Voice)
Designate one page or section for each committee member you've identified above in your journal or piece of paper. When it's their turn, you will use this

space to express what that committee member wants to share. You can do this by writing, doodling, scribbling, whatever!

Use your non-dominant hand and scribble, doodle, or draw, too. Don't worry, there's no need to ever come back to this page–it's all about releasing, expressing, and letting go–plus, you wouldn't want anyone else to read this. You are developing a new internal structure by rewiring the negative circuitry and connecting your committee members with your non-dominant hand because you want the committee members to become non-dominant in your life!

Each committee member will learn to be more comfortable communicating their feelings. Get up above it all, looking down, and observe from a safe, secure place. If you ever feel that a particular committee member is taking over, you can always imagine your inner theater, where you can walk to the 15th row where your Inner Critic sits, or back to the very last row of the theater, where you can come back to your true, authentic, relaxed Last Row perspective where you can see things with different eyes in a way that's detached yet connected, and engaged.

Then, when you are ready, you can go back to the stage or movie and continue allowing your committee members to express themselves.

When you are in the 15th row, journal with your non-dominant hand because you also want this perspective to be non-dominant.

When you are in the Last Row, use your dominant hand because you want this to be dominant.

The Last Row, or Second Observer perspective, is your place of power. It is your safe space. It's where you can always see things with different eyes. And, most importantly, it's where you can go to be safe and protected up above your committee.

Take a moment to visualize and describe the observer's perspective. Then, when you're satisfied, you can start with your first committee member and hear what they have to say.

To get the most out of this, you can visualize the committee member's conversation (or monologue) with eyes opened or closed or even write with your non-dominant hand to express childlike feelings. And remember, if it gets too difficult, go up to your observer's perspective.

Now, focus on that first committee member, and remember that we are addressing your stress and stress coping mechanism. Write everything that the committee member feels about the subject. Give your first committee member a chance to say everything they feel about the issue without judgment, criticism, or filtering. Get into the heart of the matter, feel the feelings, and express them in your journal. You are releasing and getting it all out.

Keep the thoughts of that committee member and write them down. This can be emotional, exciting, and powerful. Just remember that you can get above it all any time you choose. This is the ultimate in self-control, self-help, and self-change. It's a big key to your happiness.

When that committee member finishes saying everything they have to say, and you write it all out, take a lovely, deep, satisfying breath.

When you're ready, go to the other committee members and do the same as you did with committee member number one.

Resolve Your Committee Meeting and Finish in the Last row

Next, you will resolve your committee to help you get one giant step closer to freedom from your stress and stress coping mechanisms.

You may already feel a big release just by giving these particular committee members a chance to have their say after you've been battling with them for a long time. Now, things are out on the table. Because of all that emotional clearing, communication, support, and release, we will move into the strategy to help you resolve your entire committee meeting process. Keep your journal handy and transition out of your committee by imagining yourself above it all from the observer's perspective.

CHAPTER 7

Look down at your committee with compassion, acceptance, willingness, and appreciation, like a caring parent, a wise teacher, or the most authentic and powerful YOU. Re-read everything that your committee members have expressed from the observer's perspective and acknowledge how powerful the resolutions are from the observer's perspective.

Sometimes, the resolutions are astounding and brilliant. Other times, they are so simple, while other times, it's more about expressing those committee members just to feel better. Often, that's enough. Whatever you get, be open and receptive. Congratulate yourself. You'll go through the committee meeting again for future resolutions.

Observe Your Meeting

Now, you will experience yourself from the observer's perspective, reading what each one of the committee members had to say about your stress and stress-coping mechanisms.

It's best to read aloud with compassion and acceptance for each committee member. You may even notice that the committee members have different sounding voices and pitches. That's fine; just release, express, and be open to whatever happens. You may have noticed that you could experience your feelings differently from a new perspective, with a great readiness to change.

Now, in your journal, write down the best solutions that come to mind while you are in the observer's perspective, listening to your committee members.
You're still up above it all. Be open; let it happen. Expressing, communicating, and then getting above it all is vital.

In the future, if any of your committee members feel the need to go back into an old pattern, always give that committee member a voice and go up to the observer for a resolution.

In your journal, allow the committee members to communicate with each other. Soon, when you get stuck or triggered by stressors, you will be able to identify which committee members need a voice, no matter where you are.

Now, you can feel, express, get it all out constructively, and then get up above and outside it all with a different perspective. When you see things with different eyes, you can heal from past trauma and move forward in an enlightened state of being with compassion and acceptance. You can also let go of any bad habits or destructive patterns you've picked up to help you cope.

This powerful technique taps into your true self, creative mind, and potential to deepen your understanding of yourself and the way you've internalized your trauma. Many of my patients use it every day. Remember, whenever you are in the Last Row, you have the ultimate protection, anytime, anywhere.

Before moving on to the last step, review your committee at least five times and give yourself three days to practice and retain what you've learned. And take your time! Your understanding will deepen as you allow yourself to explore and get acquainted with your committee.

PART THREE: RELEASE

CHAPTER 8

RELEASING TRAUMA AND TRAUMA-RELATED PATTERNS

Release is where the grip of trauma, whether past or present, begins to loosen. After becoming aware of the wounds and understanding their roots, the act of releasing those burdens offers a profound liberation. It is an active process, a decision to let go of the pain, shame, anger, or guilt that has been carried, often unknowingly, inside and for longer than you wanted.

Release is not about forgetting or denying what has happened. Instead, it is a deliberate shift from being defined by trauma to reclaiming your power and self-worth. It is the pivotal point where the past loses its control over the present.

You are learning how to let go of some control to gain even greater control.

THE POWER OF RELEASE

Dr. Vincent Felitti emphasizes that the weight of unaddressed trauma often manifests in physical, emotional, and relational struggles. Releasing the pain doesn't erase the events, but it diminishes their capacity to dictate your life.

When we hold on to trauma, it resides in the body and mind as tension, illness, or chronic patterns of self-criticism. Release is the antidote, unlocking the reservoirs of self-compassion and self-acceptance that reside within.

RELEASING OUTDATED BELIEFS AND PATTERNS

Outdated beliefs are the narratives we inherit or develop in response to our early experiences, particularly those shaped by trauma. These beliefs may once have served as coping mechanisms, or ways to make sense of chaos or protect against further harm. For instance:

- "I am not worthy of being loved and I'm unlovable."
- "I don't know how to love someone."
- "I cannot let myself be vulnerable because that will show I'm weak."
- "I must be perfect to be accepted."

Such beliefs, while protective in the moment, become restrictive when also carried into adulthood. They evolve into self-imposed limitations, influencing relationships, career choices, and self-perception.

Patterns, on the other hand, are behavioral loops that perpetuate these beliefs. Examples include avoiding intimacy to prevent rejection, overachieving to compensate for feelings of inadequacy, or remaining in toxic relationships out of fear of abandonment. Releasing these patterns involves identifying and disrupting, understanding and doing the inner work to break the cycles, and learning to take better care of yourself, no matter what.

TRAUMA IMPRINTS: THE HIDDEN MARKS OF THE PAST

Trauma imprints are the physiological, psychological, emotional, and relational scars left by traumatic events. These imprints are stored in the body, mind, nervous system, and self-image, often manifesting as chronic stress, anxiety, depression, or physical ailments. Neuroscience has shown that trauma alters brain pathways, reinforcing a state of hypervigilance and/or helplessness. These imprints are not just memories; they are lived experiences that continue to influence the present.

WHY RELEASING IS ESSENTIAL

1 **Freedom from the Past:** Without release, outdated beliefs and trauma imprints dictate our actions and reactions. Letting go restores autonomy, allowing us to respond to life with clarity rather than reflex.
2 **Creating Space for Growth:** Releasing frees up mental, emotional, and physical energy that can be redirected toward personal growth, creativity, and joy.

3. **Healing Relationships:** By releasing patterns rooted in fear or insecurity, we create healthier dynamics with others, fostering deeper connections and mutual respect.
4. **Aligning with Authenticity:** Letting go of imposed narratives allows us to rediscover our authentic selves, unencumbered by the judgments or expectations of the past.

THE ROLE OF SELF-COMPASSION IN RELEASE

At the heart of release lies self-compassion. This step asks you to do the inner work to learn how to soften the harsh judgments often directed inward. Recognizing that your responses to trauma, be it fear, anger, or avoidance, were once survival mechanisms, is vital. They served you when you had no other tools. Releasing the need to blame yourself paves the way for unconditional self-acceptance.

BARRIERS TO RELEASE

The process of release isn't always linear. Resistance can often arise from fear of the unknown or a deeply ingrained belief that holding onto pain is a way to stay protected. Identifying these barriers is an essential part of the journey.

Here are some common barriers to release. Can you relate to any?

Fear of Vulnerability: Letting go can feel like exposing oneself to harm. Building trust in your capacity to cope is key.

Attachment to Identity: Sometimes, trauma becomes entwined with identity. Releasing it may feel like losing a part of oneself. Reframe this as an opportunity to rediscover who you truly are.

Guilt or Shame: Believing you don't deserve to let go is a common but misguided narrative. Counter this with self-compassion and affirmations.

Trying too hard to not be real about what you feel.

Trying too hard to not be self-critical.

THE RIPPLE EFFECT OF RELEASE

When you release trauma, the benefits extend beyond yourself. Relationships improve as emotional barriers dissolve, and you become a source of inspiration for others seeking healing.

Release is a gift you give to your future and present self, opening the door to the big step: Integration.

Remember that it is not a one-time event but a practice of continually choosing and doing the inner work to enjoy freedom over captivity and self-love over self-criticism. With each layer of pain released, you move closer to unconditional self-acceptance, setting the foundation for integration and enlightenment.

CASE STUDIES OF TRANSFORMATION THROUGH RELEASE

One remarkable case, published in the Journal of Traumatic Stress (2018), involved "Anna," a 35-year-old woman who struggled with chronic anxiety and a deep fear of abandonment stemming from childhood neglect. Anna identified and released the core trauma imprints that had shaped her beliefs and behaviors. She let go of the ingrained belief that she was "unlovable" and the pattern of overcompensating in relationships to avoid rejection.

As Anna released these outdated patterns, her sense of self-worth and emotional resilience grew. She reported a significant reduction in anxiety, improved relationships, and a newfound ability to set boundaries. Anna's journey underscores the transformative power of releasing deeply rooted trauma imprints.

Another compelling example of transformation through release comes from a study published in the Journal of Psychotherapy Integration (2020). "John," a

40-year-old man, struggled with chronic anger and difficulty forming close relationships. He uncovered a deeply rooted belief that "trusting others leads to betrayal," formed during a turbulent childhood marked by neglect.

Over several months, John engaged in practices to release this belief. He journaled, engaged in mindfulness meditation, and practiced forgiveness toward himself and his caregivers. Gradually, he replaced his mistrust with a belief in his ability to discern safe and supportive relationships. As a result, John reported increased emotional intimacy with his partner and a renewed sense of inner peace. Lastly, a patient of our very own, Judge Mary Elizabeth Bullock, wrote a memoir titled Judging Me, where she presents a compelling and harrowing case study of resilience in the face of severe childhood trauma. She rose above staggering adversity, ultimately becoming a respected trial litigator, business law professor, and federal civil-rights judge, even while navigating blindness, multiple sclerosis, systemic lupus, and several cancers.

Notably, she has an ACE score of 10—the maximum—yet her journey exemplifies the painful truth of Dr. Vincent Felitti's observation that "the body keeps the score," showing how high-trauma survivors can still achieve extraordinary success even while carrying deep wounds.

CHAPTER 9
THE PROCESS OF RELEASE

Releasing trauma can take many forms, and it is a highly individualized process. Some of the most effective methods include:

Expression: Speaking, writing, or creating art to externalize what has been suppressed. Journaling about painful memories or painting emotions that feel inexpressible can offer profound relief.

Physical Release: The body holds trauma, and practices such as yoga, breathwork, or somatic experiencing allow the body to let go of stored tension and trauma. Movement creates space for emotional energy to flow and dissipate.

Try physical release in the form of:
- Walking meditations and simply walking in nature
- Singing
- Dancing
- Boxing
- Singing
- Playing music
- Riding horses

Forgiveness: This is one of the most powerful, yet often misunderstood, aspects of release. Forgiveness doesn't mean excusing harmful behavior or reconciling with perpetrators. It means liberating yourself from the cycle of resentment and anger, freeing your energy for healing.

Letting go!

Rituals of Letting Go: Rituals provide a structured and symbolic way to release pain. Writing a letter to your younger self, then burning it, or casting stones into a river as a metaphor for releasing old wounds can make the process tangible.

Therapeutic Support: Working with a trauma-informed therapist (that has done their own trauma healing–with awareness, acceptance, letting go, supporting and being a friend to their inner judge (usually teen-age self), investing in your inner wisdom's solutions and integrating all of these into their daily life. They have to do their own work before helping others. ASK! You can guide yourself through safely releasing and resolving traumas with ACE the treatment solutions in the Enlightn app.

QUICK AND PRACTICAL TIPS FOR RELEASE

The "Breath of Freedom":
Sit in a quiet space and take deep breaths, inhaling to a count of four, holding for four, and exhaling for six.

Visualize releasing old pain with each exhale.

Repeat affirmations such as, "I release what no longer serves me" or "I am free to move forward."

The Emotional Check-In:
Spend 10 minutes daily identifying and naming your emotions and holding a Committee Meeting.

Ask yourself, "Is there something I'm holding onto that I'm ready to release?"

Write down what comes up and consider how to begin letting it go.

Mirror Work:
Stand in front of a mirror and look into your own eyes.

Speak words of forgiveness and release, such as, "I release you from the pain of the past" or "I forgive myself for mistakes made in survival."

CHAPTER 9

In the next chapter, I will share a specific strategy for releasing trauma and trauma-related patterns that I've successfully used with patients and clients for decades.

CHAPTER 10
AN EXERCISE TO RELEASE

his section will provide you with several different strategies to release your trauma on your path to enlightenment.

Some of the exercises can be done right in your own home, while others encourage you to get outdoors. Some will make you laugh, while others may make you cry.

Experiment with the various strategies outlined here, then select the ones that best suit your situation.

This process of release can be remembered as a breath of fresh **A-E-R**.

A - Asks questions that Allow you to Accept your own true nature.

E - Explores your defense mechanisms, Expresses your true wants and desires, and lets you Enjoy your life.

R - Resolves the past, Reframes the future, and respects the present.

Strategy #1: Looking Inward

Release requires letting go of your beliefs about who you are based on what you've experienced. The truth is, you are not your experiences. You are not your trauma.

So, who are you?

Now, you have the freedom and exciting opportunity to decide this for yourself. Find a room big enough to dance in.

Put your favorite song on the stereo and turn the music up louder than usual.

Ask yourself, "WHO?" repeatedly while you dance for 15 minutes.

Do this for six days in a row.

On the seventh day, turn the music down a little and, for 15 minutes, write down everything you feel.

On the eighth day, write a reminder in your calendar to dance the "WHO" for 15 minutes each week, followed by 5 minutes of writing.

Remember, you are letting go and releasing the hold your trauma and trauma response has had on your sense of identity and expression. It's time to be free!

Strategy #2: Caring for Your Physical, Mental, and Emotional Self

Set up a daily exercise program for your physical, mental, and emotional selves. Begin today. Here are some examples:

1. Physical exercise: walk, run, jump, or dance for 12 minutes.

2. Mental exercise: practice self-hypnosis, read, or write for 12 minutes.

3. Emotional exercise: laugh, cry, or write for 12 minutes.

After a few days, add the following spiritual exercises:

4. Breathe fresh A-E-R, listen to yourself, accept yourself for 12 minutes.

Follow this schedule for 8 weeks with intention, and you will find it easier and more natural. This signals that you are successfully releasing what no longer serves you.

Strategy #3: Let it Out

Find an outdoor location to let out feelings. A place to dig in the garden, kick dirt, chop wood, or throw rocks into a nearby lake or stream.

Remember what feeling is blocked and feel that feeling.

Say the words "let go" while expressing the feeling.

Dig out the feeling.

Kick out the feeling.

Chop out the feeling.

Throw out the feeling.

Experience a physical and cathartic release.

PART FOUR: INTEGRATION

CHAPTER 11

WHY HEALING IS NOT THE END OF THE JOURNEY

As you enter this final part of your journey, you must recognize a profound truth: healing is not the end but the beginning. The work you've done so far in gaining awareness, fostering understanding, and releasing the chains of trauma has been transformative. But healing itself is incomplete without integration. Integration is where your journey becomes a living, breathing part of your daily existence, shaping how you move through the world, relate to yourself, and connect with others.

HEALING AS A FOUNDATION, NOT A DESTINATION

Many people approach the healing process believing they will one day cross a finish line, a moment when the past no longer hurts, self-doubt no longer lingers, and peace everlasting. While the steps you've taken thus far have undoubtedly brought you closer to those ideals, the truth is that healing lays the foundation for something even more significant: integration.

Only through integration do you embody the lessons, transformations, and self-acceptance you have worked so hard to achieve and truly become enlightened.

In integration, healing evolves from an internal process to a way of life. It's where self-acceptance moves from a concept to a practice and from a practice to a state of being. This step allows you to weave your newfound understanding and freedom into the fabric of your daily experiences. It empowers you to live authentically, embracing every part of your story. Not just the parts you've healed but also those that continue to unfold.

CHAPTER 11

WHY INTEGRATION MATTERS

Without integration, healing risks becoming an isolated achievement, something separate from the rhythms of everyday life. Imagine a seedling that has sprouted but never been transplanted into fertile soil. It may grow for a time, but without a sustainable environment, it cannot thrive. Similarly, the insights and transformations you've gained through the earlier steps require ongoing care, practice, and alignment with your daily experiences to flourish fully.
Integration matters because:

- **It Creates Inner (Emotional) Resilience:** Healing can uncover vulnerabilities, but integration transforms those vulnerabilities into sources of strength. By embracing your entire journey, you build the resilience to navigate future challenges with grace and self-compassion.
- **It Deepens Self-Acceptance:** Integration is about aligning with who you truly are. It involves accepting not only your healed self but also the parts of you that are still growing and evolving.
- **It Sustains Transformation:** Healing is a moment of liberation, but integration ensures liberation becomes a lasting reality. It roots your growth in daily practices and perspectives that reinforce your self-acceptance.

THE ART OF INTEGRATION

This book's final part will explore the tools, practices, and mindsets necessary for integration. These include:

1 **Living Your New Truth:** How to carry healing lessons into your relationships, career, and personal endeavors.
2 **Embracing the Whole Self:** Practical strategies for accepting the entirety of your story, including the parts you would once reject.
3 **Daily Practices for Self-Acceptance:** Techniques such as mindfulness, gratitude, and intentional living reinforce your self-acceptance.
Long-Term Resilience: Building systems and habits that help you maintain your self-worth and compassion over time.

INTEGRATION AS A LIFELONG JOURNEY

Healing might feel like the pinnacle of self-discovery, but integration reveals an even more profound truth: the journey is ongoing. Unconditional self-acceptance is not a final destination but a dynamic, evolving relationship with yourself. Each new day brings opportunities to deepen that relationship, to live more fully, and to embrace life with greater authenticity.

As you embark on this final step, know that the work you've done so far has prepared you for integration and has proven your capacity for it. The tools are within you, the foundation is strong, and the possibilities are endless. Integration is not just about maintaining your progress; it is about creating a life that reflects the fullness of who you are.

In the chapters ahead, we will delve into the practicalities of integration. Together, we will explore how to weave healing into the tapestry of your life so that you can not only live with self-acceptance but thrive in its light.

This is the final step, yet it is also a new beginning. Let's take it together.

HOW TO INTEGRATE ENLIGHTENMENT INTO EVERYDAY LIFE

Enlightenment, or unconditional self-acceptance, is a profound gift that requires nurturing. Integration bridges the insights you've gained with the life you desire. This chapter is dedicated to practical strategies for integrating your new self-acceptance into daily life to become a guiding force in all areas of your life.

1. Start Each Day with Intention
Begin every morning by reconnecting with your new understanding of yourself. Use affirmations, journaling, or a brief meditation to ground yourself in self-acceptance. Reflect on questions like:

- What do I want to carry forward from my healing today?
- How can I honor my journey in the choices I make?

- What is one thing I can do today to reinforce my self-acceptance?

This intentional start sets the tone for interacting with the world and reinforces your commitment to living authentically.

Setting intentions during your trauma healing journey can shift you from feeling like a passive victim of your past to becoming an active participant in your recovery, giving you a sense of agency and direction in your healing. When the path gets challenging, your clear intentions can serve as anchors, helping you stay connected to your deeper purpose and reminding you why you're doing this important but sometimes difficult work.

Here is a specific exercise you can use to start each day with intention:

Feel Your Aura

Each morning, imagine an aura around your body. An aura is a warm, glowing light just a few inches from your body. It encloses your entire body like a soft, shining blanket that can comfort, relax, and protect you energetically. Think of it as a force field that contains positive, loving energy and keeps out unwanted negativity or stress. Only what you choose to let enter will pass through to you. You might think of this aura as made up of the radiant energy of everyone who has ever loved you, whether a parent, spouse, children, or pets. You can make your aura any color you wish or even a combination of colors.

Your aura relaxes away your stress by making you feel protected and secure. Every morning, keep your eyes closed and just feel your aura. See it in your favorite color, all over your body, warming and preparing you for the day.

Throughout the day, notice your protective aura. You can do this while driving, shopping, at home, at work, or even when doing nothing by just relaxing into it.

When you carry your aura, your imagination will unify with your body and become a tremendously positive force against stress.

Feel Your Aura in 4 Easy Steps
1. Close your eyes and imagine your aura.
2. Feel its comfort, warmth, and protective love.
3. See it in your favorite color.
4. Imagine its protection around you as you continue your day.

2. Practice Self-Compassion in Real-Time

Even with profound healing, life will present challenges. When you encounter self-doubt, criticism, or struggle, pause and practice real-time self-compassion. Remind yourself:

- "It's okay to feel this way."
- "I'm learning and growing, and that's enough."
- "This moment doesn't define me."

By treating yourself with kindness at the moment, you reinforce the habits of self-acceptance.

Here is a specific exercise to practice self-compassion in real-time:

Self-Talk

A significant discovery in psychology has been how our everyday inner self-talk shapes our lives. It's nearly impossible to feel self-acceptance and enlightenment when continually telling ourselves things like:

"I just can't do this."
"I'll probably fail."
"I just don't like me."
"I'm no good."
"I don't know what's wrong with me."
"I'll never learn."

As we now know, this is the voice of our 15th-row Inner Critic. For most people, this voice is so thoroughly programmed in their brains that these messages are all they can hear. They continually say things to themselves that simply aren't true—that they are not good enough, cannot help themselves, will not succeed, are not as good a person as they should, and do not deserve happiness. This negative self-talk is what I call being tied up in 'not's,' and it's second nature for many. Hopefully, you know what to do when this happens because of what you've learned so far!

You mustn't stop yourself from saying all the negatives; that would only give your Inner Critic more energy and control. Still, imagine how much more relaxed you could be if you were saying soothing, supportive, last-row things to yourself like:

"I'm making progress."
"I can handle this."
"I'm getting free of my stress."
"I'm willing to try."
"I know I'll get there."

Now that you understand self-talk and can identify how you speak to yourself internally, I will share a re-programming technique so you can enjoy more positive, last-row self-talk.

Say Your Name
Here is a true story: Years ago, on a teaching and learning trip to India, I met a wonderful lady who had been a house cleaner for about fifty years. One day, she had an epiphany and realized she was meant to be a mind-body healer. Everybody thought she was crazy, but she listened to herself, quit her job, and within two years, she had become one of India's most sought-after healers.

When I asked her about her favorite healing technique, she taught me the meditation you're about to learn now.

Whenever you need to reconnect with your self-compassion (and your head is filled with 15th-row negative self-talk), don't stop your Inner Critic. Instead, pause momentarily, close your eyes, focus on your breathing, and accept it. After a few breaths, say your name to yourself on an exhale, but not out loud. Do it again. Inhale, and on the exhale, say your name to yourself. Continue doing this for several breaths.

Once you're in a nice rhythm, on the inhales, say, "I accept," or "I care about," or "I believe in," or even "I love," and on the exhales, say your name. Do this for five to ten breaths. This is a last-row mantra of positive self-affirmation. Do it every day for a week and notice how much more relaxed and accepting of yourself you are. With more self-love and positive self-talk, you will find that you're equipped to show up as a better version of yourself in every area of life.

Say Your Name in 6 Easy Steps
1. Close your eyes, focus on your breathing, and accept it as-is.
2. On an exhale, say your name in your mind. Repeat for several breaths.
3. Say something loving and compassionate on the inhales, starting with "I."
4. Say your name on the exhales.
5. Repeat steps 3 and 4 for 5 -10 breaths.
6. Repeat this process daily and note how you feel and how your self-talk changes.

3. Create Rituals for Reflection
Regular reflection keeps you connected to your journey and reinforces your growth. In addition to the exercises I shared above, consider establishing weekly or monthly rituals, such as:

- Writing a gratitude journal focused on your personal growth.
- Revisiting the lessons and milestones from your healing.
- Celebrating your progress, no matter how small.

These rituals provide space to acknowledge and honor your ongoing journey of self-acceptance.

Finally, your surroundings can either support or hinder your integration.

Create an environment that nurtures your growth by surrounding yourself with people who uplift and encourage you and decluttering spaces that feel tied to past pain. Incorporate reminders of your journey into your living or workspace, such as affirmations, photos, or symbols of resilience.

A supportive environment will reinforce your commitment to living with self-acceptance.

Remember, integration is not a linear path. There will be days when self-acceptance feels effortless and others when old patterns resurface. Instead of judging these moments, embrace them as part of the process.

Remember: Growth is ongoing, not finite. Each setback is an opportunity to deepen your self-compassion and reconnect with your journey to enlightenment.

And finally, every step forward, no matter how small, is meaningful.

CHAPTER 12

EMBRACING ALL PARTS OF YOUR STORY: PAST, PRESENT, AND FUTURE

Here is an exercise I've been teaching for decades to help people embrace all parts of their story:

Get comfortable in a quiet place, take a few deep breaths, and prepare to take a long, relaxing inner walk.

As you begin, notice that you're on a great, beautiful pathway, wide enough for plenty of people to pass, but you're the only one walking today.

As you continue walking and going down a little hill, you can see the trees growing and all the branches spreading out over the pathway, creating a green, leafy canopy. It's a wonderful place. You can see the birds but hear them more than see them. You can see the blue sky through the branches of the trees and feel the sun's warmth. Here you are, with this place to yourself, and it's safe and comfortable.

As you continue walking, you notice that a huge tree is far down the path. It looks like it might be the most enormous tree in the forest. You're interested in it, and as you walk toward it, you notice some squirrels running along the branches in the distance. The clouds look pretty way up in the sky. It's one of those days you love because it's so beautiful.

Walking closer to the tree, you realize a small child is sitting by the roots at its base. As you get even closer, you know that the child looks familiar. As you reach the child, you recognize that the child is you.

What a powerful moment.

Instinctively, moved by the force of deep self-love, you and the child reach out to each other, take hold of each other, and hug each other. You feel the closeness and oneness, maybe in a way neither of you has felt for a long time. You both have this

CHAPTER 12

incredible love, care, and deep connection.

Now, a conversation can happen where the grown-up says everything you want to say to the child, offers advice or encouragement, and gives some words of forgiveness, support, or understanding. And, of course, the young child listens, totally open to whatever you want to say.

Naturally, the young child wants to say some things to you, ask questions, share sorrows, tell secrets, and reveal hopes and dreams. And, of course, you listen, fully open to the child's words. What a beautiful conversation.

After a while, you see the sun getting low, and you know it's time to say goodbye and walk back to where you started. As you reach the path and start back up the hill, you feel different, more connected to yourself. More alive, refreshed, and relaxed.

Walking back, you notice more colors, trees, and shapes in the clouds, and there's a world of difference in how much more clearly you see things.

This is a great, healing meditation you can return to at any time to embrace your past, present, and future. It's a powerful experience of communion and communication with your inner child in your wise, loving last-row voice.

To use another metaphor from nature, it's like tree rings; the growth rings inside a tree reflect each year's rainfall. There are wet and dry years in any tree's life, so some of its rings are narrow, and some are wide.

If a tree isn't doing well, you can't cut it down, carve out the narrow rings for the difficult years, and then stick it back together and expect it to live. Narrow or wide, those rings have been integral to the tree's growth and development. They are the tree.

Well, you are much the same: you can't change your past experiences, whether helpful or hurtful. They have made you what you are and are with you.

What you can do is become aware of your past, accept it, express it, and resolve the issues that trouble you. Most importantly, you can learn from your past how to take better care of yourself now and in the future.

As you reach the culmination of your journey from trauma to enlightenment, it's vital to remember that maintaining self-compassion, resilience, and enlightenment is not about perfection. It's about consistency and adaptability.

As defined in this journey, enlightenment is unconditional self-acceptance, which paves the foundation for your outlook on everything else. It's a way of being, not an endpoint. Accept that there will be moments when you falter or feel disconnected. Instead of viewing these moments as failures, see them as opportunities to return to your practice of self-compassion and resilience.

Resilience is strengthened in the context of relationships and community. Surround yourself with people who inspire and support your journey. Seek friendships that encourage vulnerability and authenticity, communities that align with your values and provide a sense of belonging, and mentors or guides who can offer wisdom and perspective. Connection reminds you that you are not alone and that your experiences are part of a shared human journey.

Maintaining self-compassion and resilience requires an openness to learning and growth. Embrace new experiences, perspectives, and challenges as opportunities to deepen your understanding of yourself. Reading books or engaging with content that inspires and uplifts, exploring new practices such as meditation, yoga, or creative expression, and attending workshops or retreats that support personal development keep your journey dynamic and prevent stagnation.

Gratitude is a powerful tool for sustaining self-compassion and enlightenment. Regularly reflect on the aspects of your life that bring you joy and meaning. Practices like keeping a gratitude journal, expressing appreciation to loved ones, and pausing to savor small moments of beauty help anchor you in the present and reinforce a positive outlook.

Life's challenges are inevitable, but a resilience toolkit equips you to navigate them with strength and grace. Build your toolkit with mindfulness or meditation to center yourself, journaling to process emotions and gain clarity, physical activities that energize and ground you, and affirmations to remind you of your worth and capabilities. Revisit and adapt your toolkit as your needs evolve.

Periodically revisit the values and intentions that guide your life. Reflect on how your actions align with your core beliefs, whether your priorities reflect your true self and adjustments you can make to stay aligned with your authentic path. This practice keeps your life purposeful and aligned with your inner truth.

Take time to honor your journey and celebrate the progress you've made. Whether through milestones or small victories, acknowledge the strength and effort it took to reach this point. Reflect on how you've grown and evolved, the challenges you've overcome, and the person you've become. Celebration reinforces your commitment to self-compassion and resilience.

The journey from trauma to enlightenment is one of courage, dedication, and profound transformation. As you integrate the lessons of this book into your life, remember that the path doesn't end here. It unfolds, offering new opportunities for growth, connection, and joy. Trust your capacity to maintain enlightenment and know that every step forward is a testament to your strength and courage.

This is not an end; it is a continuation. Your story is still being written, and the possibilities are infinite. Keep walking, keep growing, and keep embracing the light within you.

FINAL THOUGHTS

FINAL THOUGHTS

As you reach the culmination of your journey from trauma to enlightenment, it's vital to remember that maintaining self-compassion, resilience, and enlightenment is not about perfection. It's about consistency and adaptability.

As defined in this journey, enlightenment is unconditional self-acceptance, which paves the foundation for your outlook on everything else. It's a way of being, not an endpoint. Accept that there will be moments when you falter or feel disconnected. Instead of viewing these moments as failures, see them as opportunities to return to your practice of self-compassion and resilience.

Each interconnected part of this book, awareness, understanding, release, and integration, can be revisited anytime to reconnect with one's enlightened self and retrace one's steps on the enlightened path.

Before you go, here are a few reminders I'd like to leave with you as you continue on your life path: **You strengthen resilience with relationships and community.**

Surround yourself with people who inspire and support your journey. Seek friendships that encourage vulnerability and authenticity, communities that align with your values and provide a sense of belonging, and mentors or guides who can offer wisdom and perspective. Connection reminds you that you are not alone and that your experiences are part of a shared human journey.

Keep learning and growing.

Maintaining self-compassion and resilience requires an openness to learning and growth. Embrace new experiences, perspectives, and challenges as opportunities to deepen your understanding of yourself. Reading books or engaging with content that inspires and uplifts, exploring new practices such as meditation, yoga, or creative expression, and attending workshops or retreats that support personal development keep your journey dynamic and prevent stagnation.

Keep this book handy, and share it!

After all, treating the whole family is the most effective way to mitigate the transmission of intergenerational trauma (passed-down trauma spanning generations). Encourage others to heal so you can grow and move forward together.

Practice gratitude.

Gratitude is a powerful tool for sustaining self-compassion and enlightenment. Regularly reflect on the aspects of your life that bring you joy and meaning. Practices like keeping a gratitude journal, expressing appreciation to loved ones, and pausing to savor small moments of beauty help anchor you in the present and reinforce a positive outlook.

Build your toolkit to continue growing your resilience and self-compassion.

Life's challenges are inevitable, but the tools shared in this book equip you to navigate them with strength and grace. Build onto your toolkit with more mindfulness, meditation, visualization, and breathing exercises to center yourself, journal to process emotions and gain clarity, and engage in physical activities that energize and ground you. Affirmations can help remind you of your worth and capabilities, too. To learn more healing techniques and exercises rooted in ACE science, check out my other books.

Periodically revisit the values and intentions that guide your life.

Reflect on how your actions align with your core beliefs, whether your priorities reflect your true self and any adjustments you can make to stay on your authentic path. This practice keeps your life purposeful and aligned with your inner truth. Take time to honor your journey and celebrate the progress you've made. Whether through milestones or small victories, acknowledge the strength and effort it took to reach this point. Reflect on how you've grown and evolved, the challenges you've overcome, and the person you've become. Celebration reinforces your commitment to self-compassion and resilience.

FINAL THOUGHTS

The journey from trauma to enlightenment requires courage, dedication, and profound transformation. As you integrate the lessons of this book into your life, remember that the path doesn't end here. It unfolds, offering new opportunities for growth, connection, and joy. Trust your capacity to maintain enlightenment, and know that every step forward is a testament to your strength and courage.

This is not an end; it is a continuation. You are still writing your story, and the possibilities are infinite. Keep walking, keep growing, and keep embracing the light within you.

BONUS CHAPTER
TARGETED HEALING TECHNIQUES FOR EACH ACE CATEGORY

As you've learned throughout this journey from trauma to enlightenment, healing is deeply personal and requires ACE treatment solutions tailored to your specific experiences. While the four-step process of awareness, understanding, release, and integration applies to all trauma recovery, each type of Adverse Childhood Experience (ACE) creates unique imprints that benefit from specialized approaches.

This bonus chapter provides you with a customized frame and targeted treatment solutions for each of the ten ACE categories. These methods draw from decades of clinical practice and have helped thousands of people heal from their specific childhood wounds. Remember, you may have experienced multiple ACEs, so feel free to practice techniques from different sections as they resonate with your healing journey.

ACE Category 1: Physical Abuse - The Body Remembers Technique

Physical abuse leaves both visible and invisible scars. Your body holds memories of being hurt, creating patterns of tension, hypervigilance, or disconnection from physical sensations.

The Technique:

Begin by finding a safe, private space where you won't be disturbed. Sit comfortably and close your eyes.

Place one hand on your heart and one on your stomach. Take three deep breaths, feeling your chest and belly rise and fall. Say aloud: "My body is safe now. I am in control of who touches me and how."

Now, slowly scan your body from head to toe, noticing any areas that feel tense, numb, or uncomfortable. When you find tension, place your hand gently on that area and speak directly to it: "Thank you for protecting me. You did what you needed to do to survive. Now you can relax."

Visualize warm, golden light flowing into that area, melting away the old fear and replacing it with safety and peace. Continue this process for each area of tension you discover.

End by affirming: "My body is my friend. I treat it with love and respect, and I allow others to do the same."

ACE Category 2: Sexual Abuse - The Entrance-Exit Healing Method

Sexual abuse creates profound wounds around trust, boundaries, and self-worth. This technique helps you reclaim your power while processing these difficult experiences safely.

The Technique:

Imagine yourself in a movie theater watching the movie of your life. You're sitting in the last row—your safe space of wisdom and compassion.

From this last-row perspective, observe the scene where the abuse occurred, but from a distance where you feel protected. You're not trying to relive it, just acknowledge it happened.

Now, walk down to the 15th row to the place of your Inner Critic and judge. Allow this part of you to express all the anger, confusion, and hurt you feel. Use your non-dominant hand to journal these feelings, letting the words flow without censoring. Express what's wrong, how unfair it was, how angry you are.

When you've expressed these feelings fully, take deep breaths and return to the last row. From this perspective of wisdom and compassion, speak to yourself as a loving parent would: "This was not your fault. You deserved protection and love. You survived something terrible, and that shows your incredible strength."

Practice the "Entrance-Exit" breathing: Inhale acceptance ("I accept myself unconditionally"), exhale your name. Continue this rhythm until you feel centered and safe.

Remember: You can return to the last row anytime by focusing on your breathing and speaking your name with love.

ACE Category 3: Emotional Abuse - The Inner Voice Reprogramming

Emotional abuse implants harsh inner critics that echo the voices of those who hurt you. This technique helps you recognize and transform that negative self-talk.

The Technique:

Sit quietly and listen to your internal dialogue for a few minutes. Notice the voice that criticizes, judges, or puts you down. This is often an internalized version of your abuser's voice.

When you hear this voice saying things like "You're worthless," "You can't do anything right," or "You're stupid," pause and say: "Thank you for trying to protect me, but I don't need that kind of protection anymore."

Now, practice the "Say Your Name" technique:

- Close your eyes and focus on your breathing
- On each exhale, say your name silently to yourself
- After several breaths, begin saying "I accept" or "I care about" or "I believe in" on the inhale, and your name on the exhale
- Continue for 5-10 breaths

Throughout your day, whenever you catch your Inner Critic being harsh, replace its voice with your name spoken with love. You're literally reprogramming your internal dialogue from criticism to compassion.

Create new affirmations that counter the specific messages you received: If you were told you were worthless, affirm "I am valuable and worthy of love." If you were told you were stupid, affirm "I am intelligent and capable of learning."

ACE Category 4: Physical Neglect - The Self-Nurturing Ritual
Physical neglect teaches you that your basic needs don't matter. This technique helps you learn to nurture and care for yourself properly.

The Technique:
Create a daily "Self-Nurturing Ritual" that addresses the basic needs that were not consistently met in childhood:

Morning Nurturing (5 minutes):
- Look in the mirror and say: "Good morning, [your name]. How can I take good care of you today?"
- Drink a full glass of water mindfully, thinking: "I deserve clean, fresh water for my body"
- Eat something nourishing, however small, saying: "I deserve to have my hunger satisfied"

Body Check-In (3 times daily):
- Pause and ask your body: "What do you need right now?"
- Listen for signals of hunger, thirst, fatigue, or discomfort
- Respond immediately to these needs, even in small ways

Evening Appreciation (5 minutes):
- Thank your body for carrying you through the day
- Engage in one act of physical care: stretch, take a warm shower, moisturize your hands, or put on comfortable clothes
- Say: "I am learning to be a loving parent to myself"

Keep a journal of how it feels to consistently meet your own needs. Notice how your relationship with yourself shifts as you prove you're worthy of care.

ACE Category 5: Emotional Neglect - The Committee Meeting for Emotional Healing
Emotional neglect often leaves people disconnected from their feelings, unsure what they need emotionally. This technique helps you reconnect with and honor your emotional world.

The Technique:
Visualize your emotions as committee members sitting around a meeting table. Each emotion is there for a reason and deserves to be heard.

Identify which committee members are present today. They might include:
- Sad
- Angry
- Lonely
- Afraid
- Hopeful
- Confused
- Grateful

Give each committee member a voice by journaling with your non-dominant hand. Let each one express what they are feeling and what they need. Don't judge or try to fix. Just listen.

For example:
- Sad might say: "I feel ignored and want to be acknowledged"
- Angry might say: "I'm tired of being told I don't matter"
- Lonely might say: "I want connection and understanding"

After hearing from your committee, shift to your dominant hand and respond from your wise, last-row self. Offer each emotion the understanding and support it's seeking:
- To Sad: "I see you and your pain matters to me"
- To Angry: "Your feelings are valid, and I'll listen to what you need"
- To Lonely: "I'm here with you, and we'll find ways to connect with others safely"

End by asking your committee: "How can I better care for all of you this week?" Listen for their wisdom and commit to one small action.

ACE Category 6: Substance Abuse in the Household - The Baggage Release Visualization

Growing up with addiction creates emotional baggage that isn't yours to carry. This technique helps you release what belongs to others while keeping what's helpful for your growth.

The Technique:
Imagine yourself at a train station with multiple pieces of luggage around you. Each bag represents emotional baggage from living with addiction: shame, fear, unpredictability, hypervigilance, caretaking others' emotions.

Look at each piece of baggage and identify what it contains:
- The bag of "Walking on Eggshells"
- The suitcase of "Shame About My Family"
- The backpack of "Fear of Addiction in Myself"
- The duffel bag of "Trying to Control Others"

For each bag, ask yourself: "Does this belong to me, or am I carrying it for someone else?"

For baggage that isn't yours (shame about their drinking, responsibility for their sobriety, guilt about their choices), visualize loading it onto the train. As the train pulls away, say: "I release what was never mine to carry. I send this back to its rightful owner with love."

For baggage that might serve you (wisdom about addiction, compassion for those who struggle, awareness of warning signs), transform these bags into useful tools. The fear might become healthy caution; the hypervigilance might become intuitive awareness.

Create a mantra: "I carry only what serves my highest good. I release the rest with love."

Practice this visualization whenever you feel weighed down by others' choices or behaviors.

ACE Category 7: Mental Illness in the Household - The Compassionate Observer Practice

Living with someone who has mental illness can create confusion, fear, and a sense of helplessness. This technique helps you develop healthy compassion while maintaining emotional boundaries.

The Technique:

Visualize your family member with mental illness sitting across from you. See them as they were during their most difficult moments, but also as they were during their better times.

Practice the "FCC" approach by being Friendly, Caring, and Compassionate:

Friendly: Imagine approaching them with warmth, perhaps making eye contact, sitting close, or sharing something you both enjoyed. What would friendship look like even in the midst of their struggle?

Caring: Picture yourself showing care through actions by bringing them a cup of tea, listening without trying to fix, or simply being present during their difficult moments. How would you demonstrate care without sacrificing your own well-being?

Compassionate: From your last-row perspective, see their mental illness as a form of suffering they didn't choose. Extend compassion not just to them, but to the child-you who had to witness and live with this pain.

Now, create a protective boundary by visualizing your "aura" as a warm, glowing light around your body that allows love to flow in and out while protecting you from taking on their emotional pain.

Affirm: "I can love someone and still protect my own emotional health. Their illness is not my responsibility to cure, but I can choose to respond with compassion when I'm able."

Practice this when you feel overwhelmed by someone else's mental health struggles, whether in the past or present.

ACE Category 8: Incarcerated Relative - The Wisdom Letters Technique

Having a family member in prison creates unique challenges around shame, loss, anger, and complicated grief. This technique helps you process these complex emotions.

The Technique:
Write three letters (you don't have to send them):

Letter 1 - The Angry Letter (Non-dominant hand): Express all your anger, disappointment, and hurt. Write about how their choices affected you, your family, your reputation. Don't hold back. Use your non-dominant hand so the words flow without censoring.

Letter 2 - The Grief Letter (Non-dominant hand): Write about what you lost, the parent/family member you needed, the normal family experiences, the sense of safety and security. Acknowledge the person they might have been without their trauma or addiction.

Letter 3 - The Wisdom Letter (Dominant hand): From your last-row perspective, write what you've learned from this experience. What wisdom have you gained about making choices, about the justice system, about family loyalty, about personal responsibility?

Then write yourself a letter of advice: "Dear [your name], based on everything you've experienced with [family member's] incarceration, what advice do you have for living your own life?"

Listen deeply to your own wisdom. Often, going through difficult family experiences gives us profound insights about how we want to live differently.

End by burning or safely disposing of the first two letters while keeping the wisdom letter. This symbolizes releasing the pain while keeping the growth.

ACE Category 9: Witnessing Domestic Violence - The Safety and Strength Visualization

Witnessing violence between caregivers creates trauma around safety, trust, and your own power. This technique helps you reclaim your sense of safety and inner strength.

The Technique:
Begin by creating your "Inner Safe Room." Close your eyes and visualize a place where you feel completely protected. Perhaps inside a room with unbreakable walls, surrounded by people who love you, or a magical place where nothing harmful can enter.

Furnish this room with everything that makes you feel safe: comfortable seating, soft blankets, photos of people you trust, books that bring you peace, or any objects that represent safety to you.

Practice going to this safe room whenever memories of the violence arise. From this safe space, you can observe the memories without being overwhelmed by them.

Now, imagine the child-you who witnessed the violence. Invite this younger version of yourself into your safe room. Hold and comfort them, saying:
- "You were not responsible for stopping the violence"
- "You survived something no child should have to see"
- "You are safe now, and I will protect you"

Practice the "Tree Roots" grounding technique:
- Put your feet flat on the ground
- Imagine roots growing from your feet deep into the earth
- Feel yourself firmly connected and stable
- Say: "I am grounded, I am strong, I am safe"

Create a daily safety ritual: Each morning, visualize your protective aura around you. Each evening, return to your inner safe room to process the day's stresses. Remember: You have the power to create safety for yourself now, even if you couldn't control it then.

ACE Category 10: Parental Separation or Divorce - The Bridge Building Exercise

Divorce or separation can leave children feeling torn between parents, responsible for the family's pain, or fearful about their own future relationships. This technique helps heal these wounds.

The Technique:
Visualize yourself standing on a bridge between two islands. One island represents your mother, the other your father. You're in the middle, and the bridge represents your ability to love both without having to choose sides.

Look toward your mother's island. From your last-row perspective of compassion, see her during the divorce/separation. What was she going through? What pain was she experiencing? Send her compassion for her struggles while acknowledging any hurt she may have caused you.

Look toward your father's island. Again, from compassion, see his experience during this time. What was he struggling with? Send him compassion while acknowledging your own pain.

Now, focus on yourself standing on the bridge. Realize that you can:
- Love both parents without betraying either one
- Feel sad about the divorce without it being your fault
- Be angry about how it affected you while still having compassion for their struggles
- Create your own vision of relationships that's different from theirs

Create a personal mantra: "I am the bridge of love in my family. I can connect with both sides while staying true to myself."

Journal with your dominant hand about the lessons you've learned about relationships from their divorce. What do you want to do differently? What strengths did you develop from navigating this challenge?

Practice self-compassion for the child who just wanted their family to stay together, while celebrating the adult who has learned to create their own definition of love and family.

Before you go...

Practice the techniques that feel most relevant to your experiences, but don't limit yourself to just one category. Many people have multiple ACEs, and healing one area often supports healing in others.

Most importantly, be patient and compassionate with yourself. You're doing courageous work by facing these experiences and choosing to heal. Every time you practice one of these techniques, you're breaking cycles that may have existed in your family for generations.

You are not just healing yourself—you're healing the future. This is sacred work, and you have everything within you to succeed.

Keep returning to your breath, keep speaking your name with love, and keep trusting the wisdom that lies within your last-row self. You are worth this effort, and you deserve the peace and freedom that comes from healing your deepest wounds.

Your journey from trauma to enlightenment is not just possible—it's already underway.

Additional titles from Dr. Brian Alman, published by Storyteller Media, are available on www.storyteller.media:

True Sage: Oracle Cards and Guided Journey Booklet (Feb. 2026)

&

All Hypnosis is Self Hypnosis (Nov. 2026)

To explore more of Dr. Brian Alman's work, including the groundbreaking Enlightn App:

www.drbrianalman.com

Or by scanning the QR Code:

For media and booking inquiries:
contact@storyteller.media